Molyneux St. John

The Sea of Mountains

Vol. II: An account of Lord Dufferin's tour through British Columbia in 1876

Molyneux St. John

The Sea of Mountains

Vol. II: An account of Lord Dufferin's tour through British Columbia in 1876

ISBN/EAN: 9783743337459

Manufactured in Europe, USA, Canada, Australia, Japa

Cover: Foto ©ninafisch / pixelio.de

Manufactured and distributed by brebook publishing software (www.brebook.com)

Molyneux St. John

The Sea of Mountains

THE SEA OF MOUNTAINS.

VOL. II.

THE SEA OF MOUNTAINS

AN ACCOUNT OF

LORD DUFFERIN'S TOUR

THROUGH

BRITISH COLUMBIA

IN 1876.

BY

MOLYNEUX ST. JOHN.

IN TWO VOLUMES.

VOL. II.

LONDON:
HURST AND BLACKETT, PUBLISHERS,
13, GREAT MARLBOROUGH STREET.
1877.

All rights reserved.

CONTENTS

OF THE

SECOND VOLUME.

CHAPTER I.

Fort Simpson—Scene of Cannibalism—Cannibal Medicine Men—Some Indian Idiosyncrasies—Queen Charlotte's Islands—The Hydah Indians—A Deed of Vengeance—Visit of the Hydahs to Victoria—Sail-Houses—Arrangement for a Bear Hunt—Trade in Dog-Fish Oil—The Chinook Jargon—Ancient-looking Village—Curious Wood Carving—The Hydah Women 1

CHAPTER II.

A Citizen of New York State—Initiation of a Medicine-Man—A Grand Drink—The Nunpkish Indians—Search for the Medicine-Man—Education in Cormorant Island—The Indians of the Coast—Queen Charlotte's Islands—Burrard's Inlet—A Giant of the Forest—New Westminster—Reception of the Governor-General 38

CHAPTER III.

Provincial Squabbles—Journey from New Westminster to Yale—Harrison River—Fort Hope—Scenery of the Fraser River—Yale—Address to the Governor-General—Indian Interpretation of Lord Dufferin's Speech—Chinese Residents—Conveyance of Goods from Yale—Teams—Bull-whackers—Discovery of a Cropout 75

CHAPTER IV.

A Joke—Reported Dangers of the Road—A Privilege of English Nobility—Salmon Houses—Indian Method of Catching Salmon—Fish-drying Platforms—Cañons of the Fraser River—The Fraser—Hell Gate—A Dangerous-looking Road—The Rule of the Road—Courage of Lady Dufferin—Camp on Jackass Mountain 106

CHAPTER V.

Lytton—Reception of the Governor-General—Indian Gala Day—Indian Villages and Houses—Indian Graves—Lax Morality of Indian Belles—The Thompson River—Cook's Ferry, or Spence's Bridge—A Modest Indian Maiden—Bunch Grass—Trout-fishing—Arrival at Kamloops—A Master of Etiquette—Flogging of Indian Women . . . 129

CHAPTER VI.

Speech of the Governor-General at Victoria . 160

CONTENTS. vii

CHAPTER VII.

Remarks on Lord Dufferin's Address—Mr. Mackenzie—Accusations against the Canadian Premier—Unreasoning Partisanship—Menace of the Separation of British Columbia from Canada—Unpleasant Feature of the Position—Treatment of the Indians of British Columbia—Indian Reservations—United States and British Indians 230

CHAPTER VIII.

California—San Francisco—Gold and Paper Money—The Slaves of the South—The Chinese in California—Immigration of Chinamen—The " Six Companies"—Coolie Traders—Dread of Assassination—Life in a China-town—Visit to the Chinese Theatre—A Chinese Restaurant—A Joss-House . . . 241

CHAPTER IX.

Resumé of the Governor-General's Tour—Scenery of British Columbia—Mineral Wealth—The Douglas Pine—Lumbering in the Province—The Cedar—Huge War Canoes of the Northern Indians—Difficulties in the way of Agriculture—Railway Projects—Waddington—Reception at Victoria . . 275

THE SEA OF MOUNTAINS.

CHAPTER I.

Fort Simpson—Scene of Cannibalism—Cannibal Medicine Men—Some Indian Idiosyncrasies—Queen Charlotte's Islands—The Hydah Indians—A Deed of Vengeance—Visit of the Hydahs to Victoria—Sail-Houses—Arrangement for a Bear Hunt—Trade in Dog-Fish Oil—The Chinook Jargon—Ancient-looking Village—Curious Wood Carving—The Hydah Women.

WHEN Lord and Lady Dufferin had ended their visit at Metlakahtla Bay they came on board the *Douglas* and started at once for Fort Simpson, which is twenty-four miles to the northward of Mr. Duncan's mission, and a few miles south of the United States' last acquisition, the territory of Alaska. Fort

Simpson was once the principal fur-trading post of the Hudson's Bay Company on this side of the Mountains, but the prosperity of an Indian trading establishment withers as the men of the outside world approach it, and civilization is reaching even Fort Simpson. To-day the Indians of this neighbourhood are more intent upon getting to Victoria, and enjoying the delights of that metropolis, than upon hunting the fox or marten.

The Company still retain the fort in its old form, but the necessity for its high walls, flanking bastions, and closed gates has disappeared, and at a few hundred yards from its guns (which are now outside the fort for saluting purposes), are the residence and chapel of the gentleman who has succeeded Mr. Duncan in his spiritual charge of the Indians. Here the Indians had heard of the Governor-General's coming, and the guns were ready loaded to greet him. So anxious, indeed, were the Indian gunners to exhibit their artillery practice that, on Colonel Littleton's landing with the rest of the staff before Lord Dufferin, he drew one half the salute before he could stop the zealous Tsimpsean who commanded the battery.

There is a large Indian village round the fort (the houses of which are like all other Indian houses we have seen, square enclosures of cedar boards), or rather there are several Indian villages all run into one. Each of these is inhabited by a different branch of the Tsimpsean nation, who in olden times used to fight and occasionally eat one another with much gusto. One has often heard of the cannibalistic proclivities of the Tsimpsean Indians, but on investigation it does not appear that they were ever cannibals in the sense in which we understand that word. The traditional "Hokey Pokey Winkey Wum," King of the Cannibal Islands, is always supposed to have been ruler of a nation who consumed their captives as an article of diet, but the Tsimpseans regard any of their own number who may so depart from the ordinary rules of good taste with great fear and abhorrence. It seems rather to be part and parcel of the hideous mummery with which Indian medicine-men practice on the credulity of their tribe, and possibly so work upon their own imaginations as to deceive themselves.

A letter of Mr. Duncan's gives a good account of one of these cannibal scenes at Fort Simpson, and seems to indicate that the practice is, as I say, confined to the medicine-men who are always amongst all Indians anxious to mystify and terrify their friends. He says :—

"An old chief in cool blood ordered a slave to be dragged to the beach, murdered, and thrown into the water. His orders were quickly obeyed. The victim was a poor woman. Two or three reasons were assigned for this foul act. One is that it is to take away the disgrace attached to his daughter, who has been suffering some time from a ball wound in the arm. Another report is that he does not expect his daughter to recover, so he has killed his slave in order that she may prepare for the coming of his daughter into the unseen world. I think the former reason is the most probable. I did not see the murder, but immediately after I saw crowds of people running out of their houses near to where the corpse was thrown, and forming themselves into groups at a good distance away. This, I learnt, was from fear of what was to follow.

Presently two bands of furious wretches appeared, each headed by a man in a state of nudity. They gave vent to the most unearthly sounds, and the two naked men made themselves look as unearthly as possible, proceeding in a creeping kind of stoop, and stepping like two proud horses, at the same time shooting forward each arm alternately, which they held out at full length for a little time in the most defiant manner. Besides this, the continual jerking their heads back, causing their long black hair to twist about, added much to their savage appearance. For some time they pretended to be seeking the body, and the instant they came where it lay they commenced screaming and rushing round it like so many angry wolves. Finally they seized it, dragged it out of the water and laid it on the beach, where I was told the naked men would commence tearing it to pieces with their teeth. The two bands of men immediately surrounded them, and so hid their horrid work. In a few minutes the crowd broke again in two, when each of the naked cannibals appeared with half of the body in his hands. Separating a few yards they commenced, amid horrible yells, their still more horrid feast. I may mention that the two bands of savages just alluded to belong to that class which the whites term 'Medicine-Men.'"

These cannibal medicine-men are regarded as extremely dangerous, because it was never known when they might be, so to speak, on the rampage, and their immediate neighbours were frequently in extreme danger, and were occasionally compelled to take to their canoes to avoid being torn to pieces. After a while they adopted the plan of keeping a deceased slave on hand ready for immediate use. It is a curious delusion that led the young men of the village to regard as an honour, or a special boon, the loss of a mouthful of flesh abstracted between the teeth of these furious blood-thirsty buffoons.

Mr. Duncan, as I mentioned in my last letter, set himself to combat this state of things, but removed to Metlakahtla, and his place at Fort Simpson is now supplied by Mr. Crosby, a Wesleyan minister, who is doubtless well-known to many of your Toronto readers. The presence of white men, however few in number, has a great moral effect upon Indians, and by degrees the more objectionable features of

Indian life have disappeared or are rapidly disappearing about Fort Simpson. A few of the elders of the village were pointed out to me as those who had been prominent in the medicine orgies of times past, and it was softly whispered that, although denied by the Indians, there had recently been a return to the old idosyncrasies so far as an isolated case of medicine "cannibalism." Looking at their good-natured faces, and witnessing the quiet orderly way in which they live at Fort Simpson and Metlakahtla, one would never suspect that only a few years ago these people were so much more like wolves than human beings.

In appearance they are unlike Chippewas or Indians of the plains; they have more the appearance of the Islanders in the South Seas than that which is generally supposed to distinguish the Indians. They are dusky coloured, but with no tint of red in it. They have broad round faces with high cheek bones, and they have a sturdy, squabby appearance and gait,

INDIANS OF FORT SIMPSON.

very unlike the graceful movements of an Indian of the plain. All the Indians on this coast, so far as we have yet seen them, resemble one another more or less, but all retain the marked difference that exists between the coast and the interior men. We saw in a wild form at Fort Simpson that which we afterwards saw in greater perfection in Queen Charlotte's Islands; the carving in wood work about the door and posts of the Indian houses. There were a few only here who had carved images— their crests or tokens—before their houses, but there was one long pillar erected in memory of a deceased chief that was remarkable. But on the whole one was a little disappointed with Fort Simpson, and not sorry that the visit was only to be one of a few hours. The Indians are no longer attractive as being outrageous scoundrels, and they have not availed themselves very much of the white man's civilization, except to wear his clothes and when they can to drink his whiskey, and so are not very interesting from that point of view.

Of course a good number of them are now Christians, but they are a loafing, mud-larking kind of Christians, that never excite any violent admiration. A fact worth mentioning of them, as one of the men at Metlakahtla, is that on being baptised a great many of them retain, by their own express desire, their old Indian name as a surname; so that you may find two brothers, one called John Peter and the other Abraham Skooginaslake. They were all very cordial in their welcome to Lord and Lady Dufferin, and followed them into the Fort and to the door of Mr. Morrison's dwelling-place, in which the wife of the absent trader received her distinguished visitors. Here the Indian spokesman made a speech to His Excellency, which Mrs. Morrison interpreted, to the effect that all the Indians were glad to see the great chief, that the sick and aged were glad to see him also, that they were sorry that there were not more of them present, and that they would remember his visit and talk about it all the days of their lives. Probably this implied that the whole of them, sick and aged included, expected a present, and that they expected to be able to talk of his bounty all their lives. In reply to this speech, Lord Dufferin assured them of the satisfaction which he felt in visiting them, and explained the beneficent sentiments entertained towards them by Her Majesty and her Government of Canada, and told them of the advantages they would enjoy by continuing to progress in civilization and to obey the laws which were designed as much for the protection of the Indian as the white man. He then ordered the distribution of a few presents that he had brought for them, and re-embarking sailed away for Metlakahtla, where he arrived in the evening, and was met by the promised national howl from the crews of Tsimpsean canoes that had been waiting for him. Their song was the dirge for the dead sung by a returning war party. It appears to be the principal relic of their former minstrelsy and is hardly worth preserving. It is, as it is intended to be, extremely melancholy, filled with spasmodic exclamations, and calling upon the dead, but is calculated to defeat its own end by leaving it open to doubt whether the greater anguish should be felt for the loss of the slain, or in view of the fact that some had been still left alive to sing.

Early next morning the *Amethyst* and the *Douglas* weighed anchor together, and started for Queen Charlotte's Islands. This group, which lies from about fifty-two deg. to fifty-four deg., thirty min., north latitude, and between a hundred and thirty-one and a hundred and thirty-three deg. west longitude, consists of three islands, the most southerly—a very small one—being called Prevost Island, the centre island, Moresby Island, and the northern one of the group—the largest—Graham Island. They are almost one island, being separated only by two extremely narrow straits. To reach them, our course lay straight out to sea by the main shore, and steering for Skedgate Bay, a harbour at the southern extremity of the Northern Island, and thus in the centre of the group, we soon lost sight of land on either side, and were dancing over the waves of the Pacific.

Of the Queen Charlotte's Islands, very little definite knowledge has been had until quite lately. They were known to be large islands, on which it was understood there were some large open tracts of country, and in the streams of which gold had been discovered. But the inhabitants were a nation of fierce and turbulent Indians, who objected to the white man prospecting their islands, and who had given most convincing practical proof of their opposition to his presence. Several parties had landed and explored and returned in safety, but many had started to investigate the country and had never again been heard of.

The Hydahs—as that nation of Indians are called—have for years been regarded as the most to be feared of any natives on the coast. Having a strip of nearly one hundred miles of ocean between themselves and their nearest neighbours they felt secure from all attack, and building themselves enormous canoes, capable of holding thirty or forty warriors, they were wont to start out on marauding expeditions which, being unexpected by other tribes, were always disastrous and bloody. There was no security against an enemy who knew no restraining power save a south-east wind, and whose fleets of war canoes were so large, so well manned, and so numerous. Just as in olden days the Iroquois of Lower Canada swept the country with their daring deeds, and succeeded in making themselves an object of terror to the Indians westward, so the Hydahs have established a name for themselves which until the last few years was significant of murder and marauding.

It was the Hydahs upon whom a party of surveyors, in the earliest days of the colony, revenged themselves for the murder of some comrades. The Indians were accustomed to set upon any parties of white men that might come to the Island, while the latter were asleep, and the morning would rise upon the slaughtered forms scattered round the smouldering ashes of the camp fires. On this occasion, one of the party suggested a precaution. Each man taking a log of wood wrapped it in his blanket, and placed it by the fire in the position which he himself would have occupied had the party gone to sleep in the usual way. They then all withdrew into the neighbouring bushes, and guns in hand, waited to watch what might happen. In the dead of the night when the fire had burnt low, and when under ordinary circumstances every man in the camp would have been asleep, the Indians crept cautiously up to the fire. A moment's survey of the scene showed them that the white men were as usual asleep, and uttering a yell they buried their hatchets in the blanket-covered logs that lay round the fire. The next moment the guns in the surrounding bushes rang out in a volley, and the Indians fell one over another on the spot where they had struck the blows at the supposed white men. I could mention numbers of cases illustrative of their treachery and ferocity, were it not that their name stood warrant for their character.

Soon after these occurrences, Victoria sprang up from its condition as a Hudson's Bay Company's post to the central point of the business that arose in connection with the newly-found mines up the Fraser, and the Hydahs, as well as all other Indians on the coast, were eager to visit this white man's settlement. But now the recollection of their evil deeds came home to them. Not only had they been murdering white men and might be called to account for that, but as many of their predatory excursions had been along the coasts of their southern neighbour, Vancouver Island, dangers lay in that direction. Like the Danes of old, they had gone forth the Vikings of the North Pacific, and now when they wished to travel in peace they must go through the very straits and passages which they had never visited but to ravage and destroy. Their presence would be treated as another invasion, and they would be watched and set upon throughout their route. Particularly might they look for warm reprisals from the Uctetahs, who, being never at peace with themselves except when at war with other people, had particular inducements to fall upon the Hydahs; and having a large stockaded village—from which they subsequently defied one of Her Majesty's gunboats—in the neighbourhood of which the Hydahs must pass, the probabilities of having, in spite of the best intentions in the world, to fight their way down to Victoria presented itself to the Queen Charlotte's Islanders. However they were not to be deterred by this, but arming themselves and well filling a number of their large sea-canoes, they started, and after some passing skirmishes, in which a few men were killed, they reached Victoria.

Here they first came in contact with those features of civilization which are always so alluring and so destructive to the savage, and while the men surrendered themselves unreservedly to the pleasures of whiskey, the women exchanged what Swinburne calls the lilies and languor of virtue for the roses and rapture of vice, and speedily the first blows were struck that were to level the old-time Hydah supremacy. They camped close to the then small town of Victoria, and it was there that the rows and disturbances arising from their orgies created such an alarm that the necessity arose of awing them by the appearance of the Marines in their encampment, to be soon after followed by their removal in the *Tribune*, as I have already narrated.

When we arrived at Skedigate Bay on Friday, I made inquiries, hoping to learn that one or both of my old friends the Hydah Chiefs, whom, with their followers, we had cleared out of Victoria in the days that are no more, were still living, but I found that the son of one reigned in his father's stead, and that the other had come to an untimely end in a manner somewhat similar to that of the lamented Pipchin of the Peruvian mines, except that, whereas Mr. Pipchin was knocked on the head with a quart-pot, my friend received his *quietus* from the butt end of a Hudson's Bay trading gun. It was late when both ships arrived before the Indian village, and we intended to defer our visit until the next day, but Lord Dufferin was particularly anxious to go out in search of a bear next day, and Mr. Blenkinsop, the interpreter, who was on board of the *Douglas*, was required to make the necessary arrangements with the Indians; so, late as it was, we went on shore with him.

The Indian village, which we could hardly distinguish in the darkness of the evening, for the moon had not yet risen, lay in a nook exactly opposite where the vessels were anchored, but most of the Indians were away, and we were directed to pull for about a mile and a half up the bay, where a large assemblage of people were camped, engaged in making dog-fish oil, which they sold to a trader who had established himself at the point. As we turned round a rocky promontory, we saw the beach thickly covered with what the Indians call sail-houses, a species of shelter which is, exactly as its name implies, obtained by stretching a sail over a horizontal pole and fastening down the four corners. The Indians had all retired for the night, but the alarm created by the dogs and our own voices speedily aroused them, and as an Indian's toilette is easily made, and mainly consists in giving his blanket a hitch over his shoulder, we were soon surrounded by the gentlemen and by a few of the ladies of the village.

Our first business was to find what could be done towards a hunt for the morrow, and to see the proper persons we were taken to the chief's tent, which was one of the last in the double row. On our entering, a lady sleeping next to the fire hastily put some dry sticks on to the embers, and blew the red cinders into a blaze. By the light thus afforded, we could see that the tent was occupied by nearly twenty persons of both sexes and every age, all of whom were sitting up on the mats which served as beds, and were anxious to know the meaning of this visit at so late an hour. There was a very lengthened discussion of pros and cons concerning the hunt Lord Dufferin desired to make, some thinking that it would be impossible for him to shoot a bear in such a country as that in which bears were likely to be found. At length, however, the discussion resulted in the opinion that if the Governor-General were to start into the woods with the Indians and their dogs, and would go dressed as they would—merely with a shirt on—he might manage to get a shot. Still they thought this would depend on his being a spare man; they did not think that a fat man could get through the woods even divested of every hindering garment.

We had time to visit the store of the trader who was buying the dog-fish oil, and to learn some of the particulars of the trade from him. The oil is extracted principally from the liver of the dog-fish, though the women to whom the rest of the fish is given manage to get some oil from their share. The oil is extracted by boiling the fish, and then being put into tubs, is shipped to Victoria, where it sells for a sum ranging from fifty to seventy-five cents per gallon. The general effect of an Indian encampment, when this manufacture is going on, is rather dog-fishy, though the Hydahs are the cleanest and neatest Indians we have seen on the coast, with the exception of Mr. Duncan's flock at Metlakahtla. We were introduced to the residents of several of the tents, who received us with an entire absence of formality or ceremonial, they being in bed during our visit, and raising themselves on their elbows or other convenient posture to talk to us. Some of them speak English after a fashion, but the general method of intercommunication on this coast is by the use of the Chinook jargon, which is very easily learnt, and is spoken by all tribes alike.

Before going on board there was yet inquiry to be made as to the possible purchase of one of the carved posts of which we had seen a few at Fort Simpson, and of which we could see from the ship there were a number on shore. For this it was necessary to pull round to the permanent village, and as we returned round the rocky point which we had before passed, we came upon a scene unlike anything that can be found elsewhere upon the coast. The moon had risen while we stayed in the farther bay, and was now at the full, casting its rays across the water upon the Indian village. This concourse of houses, built almost in single line, stretched for some distance round the edge of the bay, the waters of which broke in silvery ripples, making a gentle splash from headland to headland. From the centre of every house, and also at a little distance out in front and in rear of many of them, rose heavy carved pillars ranging from thirty to sixty feet high standing out in relief against the sky high above the houses of which they were part, or to which they appertained. The houses themselves were partially lost to view in the shadow of the hills, but the ascending columns in their varying heights rose clear above them into the moonlight, and gave the village the appearance of an Eastern city with innumerable minarets.

As we pulled across the corner of the bay we could partially distinguish some of the carved outlines in the moonlight, and here and there, half in bright light and half in deep shadow, the long, high-prowed canoes that had been hauled up and stowed away each in the immediate vicinity of its owner's house. No dog barked as we pulled in towards the pebbly beach, and not a sign or sound of a human being was to be heard. And remembering that the approach of a stranger to an Indian village is usually heralded by all the dogs in the place, and watched by observant blanketed forms, we felt in the utter stillness of the night, and looking upon the huge carved images, such as those which one associates with Nineveh and Babylon, as if by magic aid we had been transported to some Eastern land, and as if our boat's keel were grating against the threshold of a city of the dead.

We walked through the village, from which no sound of life arose, examining as well as we could the strange weird-like figures and hideous-looking creatures that stood sentinel-like before these Indian dwellings, and had seen generation after generation of Hydahs rise, blossom, and decay. At last failing to find anyone with whom we could enter upon the required negotiation, we pulled off to the ship determined to make an early inspection of this strange village in the morning. Lord Dufferin had sent word that he wished the *Douglas* to delay her intended early start for an hour, in order that the correspondents might have an hour on shore, he himself intending to remain with the *Amethyst* for the projected hunt. So by the light of the sun, which was just showing over the tops of the hills, we went on shore to inspect the pillars and carvings of this Hydah village. It was nearly empty, the majority of the inhabitants being at or on the road to Victoria, or else with the camp in the adjajent bay.

The village consists of about forty houses, each of which contains several families, as we found to be the case in most of these Indian settlements, and these houses are built in one continuous line, some little distance above high water mark. There are a few smaller houses—or storehouses—behind the others, but that which attracts the eye and rivets the attention at once is the array of carved cedar pillars and crested monuments that rise in profusion throughout the length of the village. In the centre of the front face of every house was an upright pillar of cedar, generally about forty feet high and from two to three feet in diameter.

From base to top these pillars had been made to take the forms of animals and birds, and huge grotesque human figures, resembling somewhat the colossal figures recovered by the excavation at Nineveh. The birds and reptiles, curious and unlike as they were any the Indians themselves see, one could understand, but there were griffins and other fabulous animals represented that one would have imagined the carvers thereof had never heard of. The carvings were in some places elaborate, and in many places coloured. Some of the pillars, a few yards in front of the houses, were surmounted by life-size representations of birds or animals, the token of the family, coloured in a fanciful manner. In one or two instances there were outline carvings on a board surmounting a pillar, as a picture might be set on the top of a post. The main and tallest pillars, however, were those of which one formed the centre of each house, and through which entrance was had into the interior. Perhaps the reason for this arrangement was that an enemy would have some difficulty in storming a house which he had to enter by stooping, and from which having entered he could not retreat. Many of the rafters of the houses protruded beyond the eaves, and terminated in some grotesque piece of carving. I am not able to form an exact estimate of the age of this village. The Indians could not tell when it was begun, nor, so far as we discovered, had they any tradition on the subject. They must, however, have some legends about it, but our time was so short, and our means of communication so limited that we were not able to push our inquiries as far as desirable. The village must, however, be some hundreds of years old, for the cedar rafters in some houses were crumbling to pieces, and cedar lasts for centuries. Many of the pillars bore signs of being very old, but they were usually sound. The houses themselves are renovated or re-built when required. In one case the Indian proprietor told us the house was only two years old, but he could not tell how old were the columns against which it was built.

I can hardly exaggerate the surprise which was generally felt at this unexpected spectacle. The Indian villages are usually so essentially only places of shelter against inclement weather, that the appearance of an Indian town of such indisputable age, with such evidences of dexterity in a branch of art, and still more strange the associations which one felt existed between what we now saw and that which, in the older world, had been lost for centuries, gave rise to endless wonderment and surmise. Again and again it was asked where did the Hydahs obtain the models from which they have copied, since they never could have seen what they have carved about their dwellings. One of the party purchased a walking-stick with a small piece of workmanship on the handle, but they passed it about among themselves, and none could tell what animal it was intended to represent. The reflection arose that, perhaps, the parentage of the carving may have been in China, not only because of the peculiar dexterity of the Chinese, but more because I noticed one or two figures of a squatting Joss (the only way I can describe it), with the same leer on his countenance that one sometimes sees on the figures in a Chinese Joss-house, and the lower part of a supporting column in such buildings is sometimes a figure much resembling one or two of those that formed the base of the Indian pillars.

It seems a little strange that a place of so much interest should have escaped the notice of so many writers who have visited this coast, and of the officers who have surveyed its waters. There were two gentlemen on board the *Douglas* who knew every inlet on the mainland, but who had never seen nor heard of this village. The Queen Charlotte's Islands have been little known until quite recently, partly on account of the character of their inhabitants, and because they lie out seaward, out of the course of northward voyagers; but there is some reason to think that they would make excellent places for settlement. There are large open tracts on them, and the warm current which answers on this side to the gulf stream of the Atlantic, sweeps round in their neighbourhood, so that probably wheat and vegetables would ripen there while they would not on the mainland. Although it was early morning when we went on shore, we were soon glad to take off our overcoats, which hitherto we had usually found agreeable.

When we had passed and repassed along the village, and examined the workmanship around us, we sought out one of the very few houses that were not shut up. The mouth of a huge bird carved upon the pillar of the house formed the door, and through this we went into a large square room, in the centre of which a square had been laid off for the fire and for culinary operations, and around the sides of which a dozen or more recumbent forms were stretched beneath their blankets. A few rose as we entered, and saluted us with the Chinook word of greeting, "Klah-how-ya," which is the general salutation on this coast, but the majority of them paid little attention to us. There was one old gentleman who smiled pleasantly over the edge of his blanket at us, and when I called his attention to the fact that the sun was high up in the heavens, he looked up with an astonished air, as much as to say, "Lord bless me, so it is," and forthwith ordered his two daughters, who were sleeping near, to get up at once, and then quietly lay down himself with a smile of satisfaction at having performed a virtuous action. The young ladies evinced some modesty on being called upon to rise before strangers to whom they had not been introduced, but the old gentleman, hitching the blanket from off them, settled the question, and saved a world of argument.

Mr. Blenkinsop, the Indian interpreter, here opened the question of purchasing one of the carved pillars for Lord Dufferin, but the chief, who evidently disliked even discussing the subject, said that he did not know of anyone who would sell it. Turning from him to one of the occupiers of the house we were in, the question was put to him, whether he, or anyone he knew, would sell the pillar in front of the house, or one of the smaller ones hard by. The answer was a decided "no" for his own part, and a very confident expression that no one else would do so either. We had, therefore, as time was pressing, and an impatient whistle was sounding on board, to go off without the trophy. The disinclination to sell, however, was some evidence that some legend, or tradition, attaches to those carved pillars, and it would be well worth while, as a contribution to the annals of Canada, to carefully investigate and elucidate the history of these people, and the legendary stories that are, without doubt, attached to these wooden monuments.

During the last few years a great change has taken place in the once fierce and intractable Hydahs, and unfortunately it by no means resembles the change that, to a greater or lesser extent, is working among the Tsimpseans. The early visits of the Queen Charlotte's Islanders to Victoria gave them a taste for the debauchery of civilization, to which they have yielded themselves unreservedly, and before which they will go down like withered reeds. They have abandoned their predatory excursions, and now, taking their young women with them, they set out for Victoria, timing their visit to be there during the season when the miners are arriving from the interior. During their stay in their own homes, much of their time is spent in carving bone, slate, or silver ornaments—the latter being worn in great profusion by the women—for sale in Victoria. They have become lazy and will not work, while at the same time their greed for money is intense, so that even the virtue of their families has ceased to be respected by them, and their homes have become nurseries for the streets of Victoria.

The Hydah women are frequently of comely appearance, they are of lighter colour and better features than the generality of Indians, and they have now learnt to be careful of their complexions, and when at home daub their faces all over with red or black paint to prevent themselves from getting tanned while they are fishing. Some of those whom we saw at night, bedaubed with paint, came alongside in the morning wearing a very different appearance, and I was told that when they are in Victoria, they wear hats and silk gowns, and the various furbelows peculiar to the girl of the period. I remember them when a Hydah girl, with a crinoline on outside her blanket, struck envy to the hearts of her less fortunate sisters. But this race of people, having unusual capabilities, are falling lower and lower before the blighting effects of civilization, unaccompanied by education or good example, and unless some effort is made to save them—and they are worth trying to save—and to induce them to abandon the life they are now leading, a few camps of wretched, degraded, corrupted, and corrupting creatures, huddled together in the purlieus of Victoria, will soon represent all then remaining of the once powerful Hydahs.

CHAPTER II.

A Citizen of New York State—Initiation of a Medicine-Man—A Grand Drink—The Nunpkish Indians—Search for the Medicine-Man—Education in Cormorant Island—The Indians of the Coast—Queen Charlotte's Islands—Burrard's Inlet—A Giant of the Forest—New Westminster—Reception of the Governor-General.

THE Governor-General remained at Skidegate after we had sailed, with intent to kill a bear, notwithstanding the scantiness of clothing which the Indians declared to be essential to success, and we did not again see the *Amethyst* until next morning, when both vessels were steam-whistling themselves through a fog off the northern end of Vancouver Island. During the night we had got to seaward of our course—probably through faulty steering on the part of our wheelsmen—and somewhat narrowly escaped finding ourselves on the west coast of Vancouver Island. In the morning we sighted the *Amethyst*, and endeavoured to keep together through the fog, knowing that land must be near, although we could not see it. At last the mist cleared away, and the *Amethyst* passing us, we parted company. Then we held on our way along the northern coast of Vancouver, through the same region that we had travelled on our northward journey, passing the Island of Texada with its mountain of iron, and gradually making the high lands which a short time before we had left behind us.

As the shades of night were falling upon us, making everything around indistinct, the narrow strait through which we were passing opened out into a bay, at the further end of which we saw the *Amethyst* at anchor, and a little way beyond her an Indian village, the houses of which, strange to say, were white, as if newly painted. There was a rough kind of wharf covered with cordwood near them, and a trader's house at the back of this. Before we had reached this wharf, Ward, in one of the *Amethyst's* boats, came alongside to tell us that there had been some kind of a "fuss" on shore, for, with the usual forethought of Lord Dufferin's staff, he remembered that there were three correspondents on board of the *Douglas* so eagerly watching for interesting events, that anyone of them would have cheerfully submitted to shipwreck for the satisfaction of writing about it.

Scrambling up the precipitous wharf, we were met by an enterprising citizen of New York State, who enlightened us as to what had been going on on shore, at the same time giving us a short account of himself. He had been fourteen years on this coast, up and down its waters, and had leased the island, upon which he was the sole white man, for the purpose of cutting cordwood and selling it to the Britishers. He was quite excited about the cussedness of the Indians, his own failure—owing to that cussedness—to properly salute the gunboat, as he called the *Amethyst,* on her arrival, and the backwardness of some unknown persons to fulfil certain promises towards the amelioration of the condition of the Indians and the establishment of a school to which he could send his children. His dissertations on the several subjects were rather mixed up one with the other, but by attention, and with the assistance of two half-breed young men who were near, we managed to separate that which was interesting to us from that which was purely personal to the gentleman himself.

It appeared that a certain Indian in the village, who aspired to become a leading man amongst his people, had announced himself as a candidate for initiation as a medicine-man. At the same time the local chief had obtained some whiskey from

Indians passing north, and it came to be resolved that the pleasure of a grand drink and the business of the initiation should be combined. The latter ceremony varies amongst the several nations who practise it, but in the general run it is much the same thing. A candidate for initiation retires from all intercourse with other Indians—sometimes for twenty-four hours, sometimes for several days, and during this time it is supposed that he is in communion with the spirits, who are afterwards to be moved by his influence or intercession. Suddenly emerging from his place of retirement, he rushes about in a state of nudity through the village, biting a piece out of the arm or shoulder of anyone he happens to meet. Then he usually seizes some unlucky cur that is prowling about, tears him to pieces, and rushes about rending the bleeding limbs between his teeth. If peculiarly zealous, he will proceed to the graveyard, and, digging up a corpse, treat that as he has done the dog, which, as one of the young half-breeds said in other words, causes a most unpleasant odour about the camp. This thing continues for two or three days, when the gentleman emerges a full-blown "medicine-man" and doctor. The two terms are not synonymous, for a medicine-man, though a doctor, is quite as much a priest. In fact, personal observation leads me to believe that, when an Indian is sick, the medicine-man is allowed to go through his antics, after which the mother or wife of the patient quietly begins to doctor him with medicines extracted from roots having peculiar properties with which they are acquainted. But the medicine-man has his own dangers to encounter, for it is sometimes held that, if he proves unsuccessful in the first case which he undertakes, he is either a failure or an impostor, and this conviction frequently ensures his being knocked on the head on some convenient opportunity.

This band of Nunpkish Indians in Alert Bay, of whom I am now speaking, were in the midst of their drunken revelry when the *Amethyst* hove in sight, and numbers of them, conscience-smitten on the question of whiskey, and thinking that her appearance portended evil to themselves, had fled into the woods. It was this general levanting that had so troubled the lone Yankee, whose salute, to use his own words, " bust right up and came out a durned fizzle." The Governor-General coming ashore to sketch the village and its more picturesque groups of inhabitants had reassured the Indians, and when we came they had all returned to their houses and were engaged discussing the arrival of the two ships, wondering what it all meant, and whether it boded good or ill to them The two young half-breeds expressed great willingness to show us the way through the village, one of them appearing to be himself very anxious to see the performance continued from the point at which it had been interrupted by the arrival of Lord Dufferin. I think that from what he said he had been a little afraid to join them during the day, but now, having the doctor as it were under the guns of the *Amethyst*, he was anxious to make him exhibit himself to the full extent of his pretended powers.

The first house which we entered was the one in which the drinking and dancing had taken place, and here we found about half a dozen men and women squatting round the fire, waiting for the others to join them and renew their morning's occupation. The " Medicine-man," however, was not amongst them, so we passed on to the next house, being now as determined as our guide to hunt him up. The houses, which we visited one after another in regular succession, might fairly have been called whited sepulchres, for the lone Yank from the State of New York having heard a few days before the possible arrival of the Governor-General, had given the Indians a barrel of lime to whitewash their houses, which now looked clean and white outside, while inside they were dark, dismal, and very foul. Each of them contained four families, and all their relations, and each family occupied one corner and crouched round its own fire. Seven or eight houses were visited, and some friendly remarks exchanged with the occupants of each—who, by-the-by, were all enjoined by the young half-breed to repair to the dance-house—before we found the dwelling which contained the hero of the day.

As we entered, all uttered the unvarying salutation, "Kla-how-ya," and peered through the smoke caused by four fires, having no visible chimney severally or collectively. At the extreme upper end of the room there was a small group, a little way apart from which sat a woman holding a sick child wrapped up in a blanket, and near her a fat, good-humoured, half-nude individual with some whitewash marks upon his body and a kind of turban about his head. Like the good friars when they beheld the discomfited little Jackdaw of Rheims, regardless of all grammar, we all cried, "That's him," and so it turned out to be. He did not at all look the kind of man whom one would expect to find running amuck through the village, although we had been told that already he had bitten three people after the approved medicine-man fashion; but we stared at him, asked the Indians questions about him, and, as he did not appear to be about to do anything either funny or ferocious, we felt almost inclined to poke him about with our sticks, as visitors invariably do the wild cat in a menagerie, while he looked up at us not quite certain in his mind whether to be affronted at our appearance while he was in his mystical state, or whether to join in the joke of the thing and let us understand that he saw through it all as well as we did.

We had been told that perhaps he

would commence the rushing about again, and would, in that case, probably seize upon one of us, so that it was not unsatisfactory to find that he took the jocular view of the situation, and, so far as he dared, permitted a smile to flicker about the corners of his mouth. He evidently thought that as things had gone wrong all day this last straw—if it were the last, of which neither he nor any of the Indians seemed certain—had better be borne. But the young half-breed, our guide, was not contented with examining the doctor in a state of quiescence; he told me he was bound to see him "at it," and made a request to one who seemed the chief of the family that the doctor should go on where he had left off when the gunboat arrived, suggesting that he should come back to the dance-house. Suddenly he observed that the doctor had been trying to exorcise the evil spirits from the sick child, and at once insisted that he must " go on." He became quite earnest about it, endeavouring to egg the medicine man on as a mischievous boy incites a terrier to worry a cat. No one else, however, had any desire to see this, but, on the contrary, would probably have interfered in the interest of the sick child, so we bid good night to the party, and went away.

But while there, bearing in mind the remarks of the lone Yankee, I questioned the two young half-breeds as to the probability of the Indians sending their children to school if any missionary or teacher were to establish himself on the Island (Cormorant Island). They both said that all the Indians would do so, and were anxiously waiting for some white teacher to come amongst them. It is certain that the ignorance and horrible barbarity which they practise do not long survive the presence amongst them of a man who is there to enlighten them, and not trade with them. The atrocious barbarity of the Tsimpseans has been much ameliorated by and is disappearing before the influence of Mr. Crossby, Mr. Duncan and Mr. Collinson, and it would be a great thing if something could be done to extend the benefit of even the most elementary teaching to some of the other tribes. It is not pleasant to reflect that slavery is continued within our possessions, even though it be only amongst Indians, more particularly as the killing of a slave is regarded as a light matter, and is or recently was common as a means of satisfying some fancy or obeying some tradition.

Of late years something tending this way has been done by the Government, and a great step towards getting them all properly in hand has been taken by Mr. Laird, in instructing the recently appointed Commission to settle the question of their reserves. But a Government cannot go out of its proper sphere to do everything, and the elevation of these Indians from the hideous condition of barbarity in which they now are, requires missionary as well as governmental aid. Possibly one may assist the other. Whatever can be done within the range of his duty is, I believe, done by Colonel Powell, the Indian Commissioner here; but when one sees a settled village, such as that on Alert Bay, in such a condition as we witnessed it, and observes the tribes of Queen Charlotte's Islands deserting a splendid home to live by the practice of vice and die from the effects of gin, one cannot help wishing that some of the members who are so eager to flock through the gates of the Church would come out here and show the Indians, who are willing to be shown, that dog-feasts and medicine-dances are not really of much medicinal efficacy, and that it is more convenient to live decently than to die in a ditch.

The Indians of the coast do not compare at all favourably with those of the plains or with the Chippeways. Their perpetual life in a canoe dwarfs and distorts the growth of their lower limbs, and their way of living amongst the debris of fish is filthy and disgusting. I doubt whether they are as intelligent as any of the tribes on the other side, while on the other hand their foolish and degrading customs and beliefs are very different from any traditions that have weight with those Indians we have hitherto dealt with in Manitoba and the North-west. But they are tractable, and now entirely under the control of the white man. It is a question whether much will ever be made of them; they have not the country of their kindred across the mountains; but it would not be difficult to do something towards civilizing them a little, and if the accounts given of the interior of Queen Charlotte's Islands be true, those Indians at least might be made to see the advantage of simulating the white man in something more than his vices and his dress.

We next met the *Amethyst* in Burrard's

Inlet on Monday the 4th, from whence we were all together to start across the country to New Westminster on the Fraser and thence up to Kamloops beyond the Cascade range. Burrard's Inlet derives its principal notoriety from the fact that it is the rival of Bute Inlet in the struggle for the terminus of the Pacific Railway. If the line were brought down the Fraser it would terminate at Burrard's Inlet, and, of course, there are a great number of people who laugh to scorn Bute Inlet and Esquimalt, and point to the Fraser and Burrard's Inlet. As a harbour it has points of advantage, being superior to other places northward of it, except to the very far north, with the drawback of having an eight-knot tide in and out of its bay—a very serious drawback. In addition to that, the sand bar formed out in the straits by the flow of the Fraser is inconveniently close to the Inlet. Neither of these objections is insuperable, but both have weight.

From the land line point of view any opinion other than that of an engineer—and not all engineers are accepted—is worthless, so I shall not offer one, though when up the Fraser I will tell you what the country looks like.

Before leaving Burrard's Inlet everyone went down to a point in the bay with the Governor-General to see one of the large Douglas pines with which the country abounds brought down. It was already nearly cut through, so as to save time, and after considerable dodging about by some of the party, in order to find shelter in case it fell the wrong way, the two men who stood out on their boards ready to begin received their signal, and in about ten minutes this giant of the forest, whose height seemed never ending, came toppling over with a mighty crash, and a fall so heavy that it shook the earth in a most perceptible manner for over twenty yards round. Although not the largest tree that we saw, it was an immense one to our way of thinking. Lord Dufferin clambered up upon the stump, and stood about twelve feet from the ground, at which height he told us it was about six feet across. It measured over a hundred feet to the first branch on the fallen trunk, and by calculating the rings we found that it was an infant sapling when Columbus was a boy. At Burrard's Inlet there are two saw-mills—one in the village of Grenville and one opposite—which together turn out from twenty-two to thirty million feet a year, and export it to the South American Coast, Australia, and China. Australia is the principal market. Some little time ago there was a very extensive order from the young Emperor of China, including a demand for two sticks sixty feet long and seventy-two inches through, which were intended for pillars for a new palace, but the Emperor died and the order fell through. These two mills sometimes employ between two and three hundred hands.

The start for New Westminster was made from a small hamlet called Hastings, a little up the Inlet, to which place the New Westminster people had sent carriages to take the Governor-General. The road between the two places is about nine miles, and is through the heart of a pine forest. It was very hilly and very dusty, and descends upon the town by a height commanding a splendid view of the Fraser. New Westminster itself is situated on a shelf overlooking the Fraser River, which rolls at some distance down beneath the long main street of the city. We could hardly tell what the town looks like on ordinary occasions, for the inhabitants had so exerted themselves to receive the Governor-General and Lady Dufferin that the city proper looked like the least part of what we saw. There was the same tasteful display of intermingled pines and bunting which we had seen at Victoria in such profusion, and beyond the last of the arches and welcoming mottoes on private houses was a series of evergreen buildings, the central one of which was carpeted and provided with an inner bower, elevated on a dais, lined with lace curtains, and furnished with handsome armchairs, as a reception-room for their Excellencies. Another evergreen structure had been raised by the Indians, who had placed over its portals the motto, " Welcome to our Great Chief." There were several others, including one on which an inviting luncheon, had been spread, and here (in the general locality, not in the luncheon tent,) were assembled those whom New Westminster most respects and most admires.

Their Excellencies dismounted from their carriage, having been cheered half-way along Main Street by the populace, and rung in by the chimes in the tower of a neighbouring church, and took their place in the lace-appointed bower, Lady Dufferin having to arrive at that point over a path strown with flowers by the young girls who had assembled to greet her. At the same time the Volunteer Company, who had escorted them from their first entrance into the town, presented arms, the crowd again cheered, a salute was fired from a battery in front of the Pavilion by a most creditable-looking battery of artillerymen, and there was a general excitement and warmth of welcome which could hardly have been expected from a population so limited in numbers. Lady Dufferin having been presented with an address by Miss Macaulay and a bouquet of flowers by Miss Webster, two young ladies of whose names mere mention is sufficient in New Westminster, the Mayor of the city presented His Excellency with an address, and then introduced the members of the Corporation and the principal ladies and gentlemen of the neighbourhood.

The address from New Westminster was as follows :—

"To His Excellency the Right Honourable Sir Frederick Temple, Earl of Dufferin K.P., K.C.B., P.C., Governor-General of Canada, &c., &c., &c.

"May it please Your Excellency:—

"In the name of the people of New Westminster city and district, I have the honour most respectfully to approach Your Excellency with assurances of our devoted loyalty to the Person, Throne, and Government of Her Most Gracious Majesty the Queen, and to Your Excellency as Her Majesty's representative.

"It is also my pleasing duty to convey to Your Excellency and to the Countess of Dufferin our sense of the high honour which has been conferred upon us by the visit of Your Excellencies to this remote Province.

"We trust that this visit to the Western Gate of the Dominion will be a source of gratification to Your Excellencies, and that you will carry back with you to

Eastern Canada pleasing recollections of British Columbia; and we beg most respectfully to assure Your Excellency that among us the Earl and Countess of Dufferin will ever be remembered as having added fresh lustre to the Canadian name by the frank and cordial manner in which Your Excellencies have ever identified themselves with the interests, the hopes, and the pleasures of the people among whom Your Excellency so worthily represents the beloved Sovereign of these realms.

(Signed) "T. R. McINNES.
"Mayor of New Westminster.'

To which the Governor-General replied:—

"Mr. Mayor,
"I beg to acknowledge with many thanks the address which you have presented me, on behalf of the people of New Westminster city and district, and

in reply I desire to assure you that, as Her Majesty's representative, I fully appreciate the universal loyalty exhibited throughout this beautiful Province towards the Government, Throne, and Person of the Queen.

"I have also to thank you most heartily for the very kind welcome with which you have greeted Lady Dufferin and myself on our arrival amongst you.

"Having just returned from a survey of the magnificent coast line which forms the western boundary of the Dominion of Canada, we now propose to penetrate through the Cascade Range into the interior, and I have no doubt that our gratification in this second portion of our progress will quite equal that which has been afforded us by our trip northwards.

"I need not assure you that I have always taken the liveliest interest in the welfare of British Columbia, and that nothing shall ever be wanting upon my part to promote the interests and to forward the views of the inhabitants.

"We have been everywhere received with the greatest cordiality and kindness, and we should be indeed ungrateful if we did not carry home with us the most pleasant reminiscences of this conntry and its people."

Then followed addresses from the representative men from the several townships and settlements in this neighbourhood of the Fraser River to all of which Lord Dufferin replied in his usual happy and complete manner.

During the time of the reception of these addresses we heard great shouting and firing of guns approaching nearer and nearer the platform which the pavilion overlooked, and presently two large fleets of gaily-dressed canoes went singing, firing, paddling along the river bank. They reappeared shortly, as I will mention. But in the meantime some more addresses were presented to the Governor-General. A gentleman read out an address from the Good Templars of New Westminster—who, by the way, had raised a beautiful arch, on which were the words in white flowers, " Good Templars welcome the Earl and Countess of Dufferin"—and in reply Lord Dufferin said :—

" Gentlemen,

" As the representative of Her Majesty the Queen I beg to return you my very best acknowledgments for your loyal address, at the same time that I express to you my own and Her Majesty's acknowledgments for the kind welcome you have extended to us personally.

" I am fully alive to the many evils attending upon the abuse of spirituous liquors, especially in a climate which, like that of Canada, seems to invest their intoxicating properties with additional energy, and I am glad to think that the justices of the Supreme Court should exert the influence and the respect which their counsels so properly inspire to check and discountenance the evils flowing from this source. In conclusion, allow me to assure you that I shall always entertain the greatest solicitude for the welfare and prosperity of the inhabitants of this Province."

By this time the Indians were preparing to pay their respects, and their approach was heralded by the sounds of military words of command given in the Indian language. They formed a long procession, which was headed by a band of Indians from St. Mary's Catholic mission, carrying banners, whose injunctions pointed to a combination of morality with enterprise. Following this band came a long array of Indian volunteers. Curiously enough the greater number of them were dressed in the cavalry jackets of U.S. troops. This led to inquiries, the answers to which threw considerable light upon the manner in which the Treasury of the United States is swindled by Government officials, and the care which is taken to cover up the tracks that are left in the perpetration thereof.

The pow-wow that ensued upon the introduction of the Indians was, if lengthy, at least full of good assurances. His Excellency's reply, while conveying the sentiments which Her Majesty and Her Government feel towards our fellow-subjects of the native races, laboured under the slight disadvantage of requiring five different translations, which were made sentence by sentence in order that different chiefs and their followers might understand. This kind of public address has its advantages, but is a little trying to the patience. But Lord Dufferin has great patience, and never appears to be wearied in the midst of what must be very trying work. As for Lady Dufferin, her energy is no less remarkable than the pleasure she exhibits in doing what to a lady is really hard work. A dusty drive of nine miles over a series of risings and fallings is in itself something that suggests "a spell" and vinous recuperation; but Lady Dufferin, seeing hard work ahead, went straight at it without halt or hesitation, and for at least three hours was busily engaged doing it all as pleasantly and cheerfully as if it were all the newest kind of delightful sensation. One often growls at having to do some duty which one thinks might be easily dispensed with, but the example set by the lady who at present presides over Canadian society ought to shame many from ever again approaching a duty with any other intention than that of cheerfully and satisfactorily performing it.

There was then an Indian regatta, and after dinner, which no one succeeded in obtaining until past seven o'clock, for everything was subordinated to the welcoming the Governor-General, one of the prettiest sights I have ever beheld was seen on the river. A large fleet of canoes—the combined fleets of the morning's demonstration—still dressed with their masts and flags, but now brilliantly lighted by pine torches, shot out from several points into the stream. They were full of men and women, some of whom paddled, while others held aloft the blazing torches. On mustering in the river they began a song of peace, commencing to paddle at the same time, and rushed by the steamer, on board of which we were, apparently one mass of fire and flags. Then the steamer moved out into the stream placing the fleet of canoes between herself and the shore, and so showing the torchlight at a little distance. The canoes seemed to be led by an Indian distinguishable from the others by his red coat and gold laced hat, who with a picked crew in a racing canoe—which is differently shaped from the rough weather canoes—dashed ahead at every fresh movement or alignment that was made

One chief had had his two canoes lashed together and a platform constructed over them. On this he had mounted a gun, with which he saluted the Governor-General at intervals. As we went out into the stream the canoes formed into three lines, the torches now looking, as they danced upon the river, like animated bouquets of fire. At the same time a bunch of similar fire bouquets appeared at the other end of the street leading and open to the river. These, rapidly spreading out into a line, went skipping along the margin of the river, and increasing in numbers every minute, made the line more extended and more thickly studded with the dancing bunches of fire. Some of the principal houses and stores along the upper street were illuminated; so that there was a terrace of stationary light, beneath it the extraordinary phenomenon of a thick line of dancing fire-bouquets having no visible connection with anything, and then in the foreground the mass of glanc-

BRILLIANT RECEPTION. 69

ing, dipping, rising, Brobdingnag stars that were filling the air immediately above the canoes full of shouting, singing, cheering Indians. There was a band on board the steamer and another in a canoe, together with the singing and cheering, filling the air with their reverberations. The citizens were in numbers along the river, and everybody and everything seemed to be moving and taking part in the excitement. Even the rush of the river might be taken as part of the picturesque hub-bub, so swiftly did it flow and dash itself into spray against the bows of the boats, canoes, and steamer; only the grand moonlit hills that back the Fraser rested in dignified serenity. When some one on board said that their town only numbered six hundred white inhabitants, I thought he was jesting; for by the bustle, the excitement, the general uproar of welcome, and incidents appertaining to the reception, one naturally imagined that the inhabitants must have numbered some thousands. But it was done by what Lord Dufferin once called "haustum longum, haustum fortem, et haustum omnes simul" by a long pull, a strong pull, and a pull altogether, and with the aid of their Indian friends the inhabitants of New Westminister succeeded in receiving the Queen's representative in a style as wonderful as it was worthy of admiration and praise.

While yet the excitement continued, and while still the sensation of not knowing which was head and which was tail remained, a deputation of citizens came on board to deliver to His Excellency the following document on the subject of the great question—the Pacific Railway. It shows that of which we saw some indications immediately on our arrival at Victoria —viz., the difference of opinion that exists between the mainland and Vancouver Island:—

MEMORANDUM.

Conveyed to Lord Dufferin by a Deputation of the citizens of New Westminster and District, during his Lordship's visit to this city:

" 1. We beg to assure your Excellency of your hearty welcome in New Westminster and the Mainland, and trust that your visit may be productive of pleasure to your Excellency and Lady Dufferin.

" 2. That we regard your Lordship's visit to the Mainland as likely to effect the only sure solution of the differences between the Province and the Dominion.

" 3. The people of this district are unanimous in the feeling of pleasure with which they regard the setting aside of the proposition known as the " Carnarvon Terms," confidently hoping that a new proposition will be more beneficial to the interest of this Province and the Dominion generally.

"4. While patiently awaiting the final settlement of the subjects at issue between this Province and the Federal Government, particularly in regard to the adoption of a route for the railway, we would request that a thorough survey of the Fraser Valley be made before the question is finally settled.

"5. We wish also to impress on your Excellency that a very strong feeling exists at the injustice that has been done this section of the Province by the continued delay in making a location survey of the Fraser River route, which has been promised on more than one occasion, and we would consider a great wrong would be done to the settled portion of the Mainland by the selection of any other route until the Fraser River route has been thoroughly surveyed.

"6. We consider that the best and only way to adjust our differences is commencement of railway construction on the Mainland and compensation for delays.

"7. That in estimating the amount of compensation to be given to the Province, your Excellency's Government will take into consideration the great loss caused to the Mainland, no less than to the island, by the delays in Railway construction.

"8. That we desire to express to your Excellency our disapproval of any threats being held out of separation from the Dominion, as we feel that such a course is unworthy of an intelligent and loyal community."

By the time the deputation, the members of which had some private conversation with Lord Dufferin, had departed, night had well settled in, the canoes had carried their loyal occupants to their ranches, the citizens had departed to their homes; even the Chinese gongs, which had been going all day, had ceased, and all was once more quiet and at rest. Then Lord and Lady Dufferin, late as it was, went out fishing, and assisted in the capture of a large sturgeon and several salmon.

CHAPTER III.

Provincial Squabbles—Journey from New Westminster to Yale—Harrison River—Fort Hope—Scenery of the Fraser River—Yale—Address to the Governor-General—Indian Interpretation of Lord Dufferin's Speech—Chinese Residents—Conveyance of Goods from Yale—Teams—Bull-whackers—Discovery of a Crop-out.

THE *Royal City*, with the Governor-General and the whole of his party, left New Westminster at midnight, 5th September, and started on the journey up the Fraser. The first thing that greeted one's eyes in the morning was the morning paper, the "Dominion Pacific Herald," which was published late last night in time for the boat. That journal confirmed the impression, derived from the memorandum delivered to the Governor-General, that British Columbia, as distinguished from Vancouver Island, sees the Pacific Railway question with the dependent issues of compensation for delay, as well as the " Carnarvon Terms," in quite another light than that in which it is viewed in Victoria. Speaking of British Columbia and Vancouver Island as two places may be cavilled at, since they are politically one; but their sentiments regarding the Pacific Railway are far apart, and if the two places are verily one, the whole, instead of a part, must of course be heard on any question of compensation. The mainland British Columbians do not wish the Carnarvon Terms to be carried out, for they think their suggestion in the first place was ill-advised, and they repudiate the idea of a compensation which is to compensate the Island only. I have heard it stated that any money compensation that might be given would be injudicious, by reason of the contention to which it would give rise amongst the local politicians, and the pressure that would be brought upon the Government for its immediate distribution in a manner more calculated to enrich individuals than to effect any good to the Province, or even to confer any benefit on the community in general.

One of the things which is striking in British Columbian affairs is the general distrust exhibited, and tone of disparagement used, amongst men in speaking of their local political leading men on either side of the dividing fence. They seem to think that the country is over-crowded with rulers and guides, and that the people are used as counters in a game between two small knots of politicians. The Government is thought to be weighty and cumbrous for so small a population, and Mark Twain's epigrammatic satire, touching the folly of using the machinery of the *Great Eastern* to run a sardine box, is applied to the circumstances of this

Province. They are all very much behind the scenes in their own little theatre, and in their annoyance frequently feel as if they would like, were it possible, to pull down the building and construct another more adapted to their means and requirements. Too much time and public money is spent, they think, in politics which have no other object than the victory and consequent aggrandisement of one or other of the two small groups of politicians. A money compensation cast into this group would, it is thought, be a magnificent windfall for a larger or a smaller number of persons, as the case might be, but for the Province at large would be of little advantage. The compensation, therefore—think those whose opinions I have indicated—should be something not divisible by, or amongst, those who may at the moment chance to be above in the scramble for the distribution of Federal supplies. This chronic provincial contention has for some time surged round the question existing between British Columbia and the other conjoined Provinces of the Dominion. The principal scene of the local political contest is in Vancouver Island.

Vancouver Island has been promised, by the " Carnarvon Terms," the construction of the railway from Esquimalt to Nanaimo; therefore, any party desiring to re-arrange with Canada and to set aside the " Carnarvon Terms" fights in a locality hostile to any conciliatory measures they may desire to propose, while their enemies —for the word opponents is hardly strong enough to convey the character of the contest—have only to oppose anything and everything, except that which has been virtually declared out of the question, to acquire the support of nearly all the Island politicians, and one or two of the mainland who for other reasons are with the opposing power. The knowledge, informally acquired, that the Nanaimo and Esquimalt Railway would not be built, set the "Standard" newspaper afire with indignation, and induced its editor to state explicitly that separation must and should be the result of his disappointment. Fortunately his language was so violent and his insult to the Governor-General so gratuitous, that he frightened even his own friends at the outset, and it may be that the firm position and outspoken views of the mainlanders will have the effect of inducing the islanders to see that their demands are wholly selfish, and that as they are not the whole of the Province, they must shape their conduct in a measure by that of their neighbours if they wish to be heard at all.

In the meantime the location of the railway is to be determined, and so irreconcilable are the views of the two sections of British Columbia, that no government in the world can hope to make any reasonable arrangement as to the route that is likely to meet the views of both. Considerable stress has been laid on an Order

THE MAIN CONSIDERATION. 81

in Council—passed in the late Government's time—determining the locality of the terminus, as well as the "Carnarvon Terms," the sanctity of Government pledges, the necessity for keeping promises, and so forth; but while admitting the strength of all these considerations under ordinary circumstances, one is inclined to think, after seeing this country, that they have but feather weight after all, and that it is justifiable to urge that, in view of the gigantic work which Canada is about to perform, pledges or promises given, without full knowledge, ought not to be considered binding on a government, and that the most practicable and judicious route for the road is the consideration, and the only consideration which should be allowed to have any determining influence. And as the island will be disgusted if the mainland is satisfied, and *vice versa*, a statesman having no undue partiality for either will satisfy one portion of the Province, and will probably have with him the sense of the whole of the rest of the Dominion in putting aside every argument which does not go to prove the superiority of the desired direction.

The journey from New Westminster to Yale is done by steamboat up the Fraser River. The river is swift, and in some places narrowed by sand-bars. The passage (one hundred miles) is made up stream in about twelve to fourteen hours, and of course in a much shorter time down from Yale to New Westminster and on to to the mouth, twelve miles beyond. The river runs through a series of mountain ranges, and on either side is a low level flat of small but varying breadth, which is more or less covered with deciduous trees. At about fifty miles above New Wesminster, the "Harrison" River joins the Fraser. Numerous deltas and small islands have been formed at various points by the streams from the neighbouring high land, and the river wears the appearance of changing its channels more rapidly than rivers in rocky countries are usually found to do. The interior of the country in the neighbourhood of the Harrison River is quite unlike that which one would expect to see on either side of the Fraser. One sees nothing but a heavy growth of pines, but there is a large tract of open country of excellent farming land commencing at a very short distance from the river, and it will probably be found, so I am told, when there are more people to spread about this vast range of mouutains, that there are more valleys of a similar character.

Thirty miles above Harrison River is Fort Hope, a Hudson's Bay Company's post, and the residence of, amongst other people, Mr. Dewdney, the M.P. in the Dominion House of Commons for Yale district. This little place was very prettily decorated to welcome the Governor-General, who with Lady Dufferin, and accompanied in fact by every one on board, went on shore to accept the compliment offered. Lady Dufferin was welcomed on behalf of other resident ladies by Mrs. Dewdney, to whose house she went while Lord Dufferin was there. There was a general rush on the part of other people to buy furs, but neither at Hope nor at any other post which we have yet seen on this side are the furs equal to those which come into Manitoba from the north and north-western districts, nor are those which Thunder Bay merchants purchase from the Keewatin Indians.

Having left Hope the steamer continues an uninterrupted journey to Yale. Of the scenery of the Fraser River I would gladly say nothing, in order to avoid the task of attempting to describe that which beggars all mere verbal description, and requires to be seen in order that it may be realized. It is not that its mountains are lofty, grand, and sublime—though on these grounds alone it is a river of rivers

—for were its beauty dependent upon these characteristics alone, we, at least, so recently returned from the north, might have made unfavourable comparisons with Bute Inlet. But whereas at Bute Inlet the mountains rose abruptly from the water on either side in two straight, rugged, uninviting walls, the mountains of the Fraser were just far enough from the river-side to lose the harsh appearance too great closeness gives, and being seen from the winding river, presented a variety of soft lights and tints which in the case of close proximity would have appeared only as deep shade and glaring light. And going up the Fraser you see these mountains not only sufficiently close on either side, but also in a continuous succession of spurs and peaks, which appear and disappear as the turns of the river open up new vistas before you. Sometimes, as at Fort Hope, the view on every side is shut in by the mountains, and in such a case, where every mountain has its own individuality not to be mistaken for that of its neighbour, and the shade of each passing cloud is caught, coloured, and laid upon the mountain side, the scene appears to be one beyond excelling. But it must, of course, be seen to be thoroughly appreciated, for no painter can place his spectators in the same atmosphere as that in which they see the Fraser River, and art cannot supply the same effects that are produced either on the spectator himself, or on the scenery upon which he gazes, by those subtle powers which nature reserves to herself. Still it is much to be desired that Mr. Verner, Mr. O'Brien, Mr. Cresswell, Mr. Armstrong, or some other Canadian painters, would avail themselves of the opportunities that are offered in this region, and add to the rapidly developing collections of Canadian scenery some pictures of spots in British Columbia.

Yale, which we reached in the afternoon, is a small mining-trading town, built by the side of a Hudson's Bay fort. It is at the head of navigation, and in the Fraser River mining excitement did a large business. Now it is very quiet, and does a small but steady business with miners, packmen, teamsters, and such heterogeneous customers as it can find. It had turned out bravely to receive the Governor-General, not only gaily ornamenting its one street, but even decorating its outlying bridge and one thoroughfare that will be a street some day if it lives. Yale, however, is more important than it looks, for it is the centre of business of a large tract of country which is not seen from the river, and the people of which are not so much in the habit of hanging about the towns as they would be in the east.

At Yale the following address was presented to the Governor-General:—

" To the Right Honourable Sir Frederick Temple, Earl of Dufferin, Viscount and Baron Claneboye of Claneboye, County Down, Governor-General of the Dominion of Canada, &c., &c.

"May it please Your Excellency,

"The inhabitants of Yale, British Columbia, approach Your Excellency as representative of our beloved Sovereign Her Majesty Queen Victoria with feelings of sincere loyalty and attachment, and most heartily welcome you to our town. Although distant—and at present unfortunately isolated—from the rest of the Dominion, yet we have watched with interest and admiration Your Excellency's career since assuming your exalted position.

"We fully appreciate the honour of Your Lordship's visit to this Province, and with pleasure recognize your desire to become personally acquainted with the places and people under Your Excellency's benign rule. Such an acquaintance and knowledge, we feel assured, will result in our mutual benefit.

"We would also extend right hearty welcome to your esteemed lady the Countess of Dufferin, and we trust that your sojourn amongst us will prove a time of unalloyed pleasure."

In reply to this the Governor-General said that it gave him great pleasure to receive the address just presented, and also to express his satisfaction with the assurances of the people's sincere loyalty to Her Majesty's throne and person. He had always taken great pleasure in becoming acquainted with the people of all parts of the Dominion, and was glad to find the hardy pioneers of civilization in these distant regions second to none in those characteristic feelings and sentiments which were the support and mainspring of a great nation. He then thanked them for their kind expressions of feeling towards Lady Dufferin and himself, and assured them that it would afford him great pleasure to promote their welfare and prosperity by any means in his power.

His Excellency had been received by a guard of honour of the resident Indians, which he inspected, and this body of natives, who are trappers, troops, tripmen, or travellers, as occasion may require, having completed their military duties, addressed the Governor-General through the medium of their chief, who was greatly assisted by the timely promptings and suggestions of his wife. Lord Dufferin replied to this speech—which was simply an exposition of the goodness of the Indian tum-tum, or heart—in a few appropriate sentences, which he spoke to the interpreter whom the Indians had supplied from their own number. But what a language for oratory is the Fraser River tongue! The few words which Lord Dufferin had said, when handled by this gifted savage, became an oration that Burke might have envied, and some even of our own time might have in vain sought to emulate. There was no prospective termination to it; sentence followed sentence, exhortation succeeded explanation, until it really became interesting to speculate upon what he might be putting into the mouth of the Governor-General. One of my neighbours in the crowd informed me, "There's no let up in him once he's started," and it really looked as if the Indian had determined to make the most of his opportunity, and, having entrapped a Governor-General's endorsation, had concluded, as my neighbour remarked, to "orate considerable." But the driver of Lord Dufferin's carriage, seeing an opening, whipped up his horses and left the Indian with his friends to moralize over the vanity of vanities, as exemplified in the slippery nature of Governors-General.

At Yale the ubiquitous Chinaman had erected a pagoda-like, lantern-hung arch, with a welcoming motto; and the resident "John" of most decided eminence, surrounded by the many whom he represented, and mounted on a carpeted platform, read out from a roll of red paper covered with Chinese characters, in a sing-song voice that sounded like the tolling of different sized bells, the following address :—

" Yung a tung a lung tung chutpse Souchong,
  Chop it up with chopsticks chou-chou chang;
  Opium in a junk full birds'-nests couchong
  Drinking cups of Hyson, buskey bang, &c."

I won't be quite sure that these were the exact words that the amiable old Chinaman employed, but they sounded a good deal like what I have written, and the sense being interpreted is as follows :

" To His Excellency the Earl of Dufferin, Governor-General of Canada.

" We, the Chinese residents of the town of Yale, B.C., beg to approach Your Excellency, as the representative of the Queen of England in the Dominion of Canada, with the offer of a sincere welcome to this town, and that you will carry back none but good and happy reminiscences of our people and your visit to this Province on your return to the seat of Government."

To which His Excellency replied :—
"Gentlemen,
"It is with especial pleasure that I accept an address from the Chinese subjects of Her Majesty at this place. Whereever I go I receive the best reports of the Chinese residents as regards their industry, sobriety, orderly conduct, and loyal obedience to the laws; and I am glad to think that their European fellow-subjects of British Columbia should invariably treat them, as I understand to be the case, with the friendly courtesy and generous good feeling which should prevail in a community where impartial justice reigns supreme, and none of us can afford to consider ourselves independent of each other's help in developing the resources and promoting the prosperity of the Province."

Lord and Lady Dufferin drove after the reception to the house of Mr. Oppenheimer—an eminent merchant of British Columbia—where they stayed for the night, and the rest of the party made such other arrangements as best suited their convenience, in anticipation of an early start up country by coach in the morning. We spent the few remaining hours of the evening in making such purchases as were necessary for our journey, securing means of conveyance to Kamloops Lake—for we had missed the weekly stage—inspecting the town, and interviewing "John," and then made anxious inquiries at the very last moment touching the probabilities of the weather on the morrow.

Yale is the place of starting, not merely for Kamloops and the North Thompson to Tête Jaune Cache, but for Lilloet, the Cariboo Mines, and other localities, the roads to which branch off from the Kamloops route. It is the head of steamboat navigation on the Fraser, for the shoal waters begin immediately above it, and the traveller is here obliged to abandon all kinds of water conveyance and take to the mountains. The evidences of this are at once apparent. The river narrows at once, and disappears into a cañon, while in the street and about the neighbourhood one sees either a train of pack mules about to start, or another, dusty and weary, just arriving, or, perhaps, a miner's drove of mules and horses picking their steps down the bank of the river to water, following some one or two sagacious belled animals, or possibly a large, double-waggoned "bull-team," heavily laden with goods for the interior.

All the goods required at the mines, in the stores of the interior, in the wayside stopping places, and in fact wherever used, are carried over the mountain road on the backs of pack-animals, or in the heavy, lumbering waggons of the bull-whackers. In a horse or mule train each animal carries from three to four hundred pounds, even three hundred being a good pack, and the train travels from twelve to sixteen miles a day. Many of the pack trains belong to the Indians, and nearly all are driven by them. The women take part in the work, and even a very small boy or girl can assist in keeping the mules up in their places by whipping, yelling, or throwing stones at them. At night the train camps on some convenient place in the immediate vicinity of the road, where every one sees his pack-saddles carefully arranged in line, that confusion and delay in the morning may be avoided.

The freight on goods is high, varying, of course, according to the distance packed, but wages, food, and everything is dear, and in a peculiar way the dearness of freight keeps up the price on the road, while the high prices to be paid for wages, keep, hay, &c., keep up the tremendous charges for freighting. The men who are employed in freighting on this road are well paid for the six months during which it lasts. A stage-driver receives from eighty to one hundred and twenty-five dollars a month; a bull-whacker (all oxen are bulls in this country), about one hundred dollars and his rations; and even "John's" much abused cheap labour is rewarded at the rate of from thirty to forty dollars a month, and sometimes, as in the case of the cook at a stopping place, a great deal more. An Indian receives about a dollar a day when engaged for a length of time, but as a rule they prefer taking short-time jobs for which a specified remuneration has been arranged. Everything is correspondingly dear, each meal costing a dollar, and a bed the same. This seems to be the price all west of the Rockies, beyond which even the smallest pint-bottle of beer is half a dollar, and anything in the shape of "a drink" a quarter, or, as here called, "two bits." They have throughout the western slope this imaginary coinage of a "bit." It arose in the days when payments were really made in bits of precious metal, and it has survived the introduction of regular coin, principally I think because any irregular defined value is always most favourable to the store and saloon-keepers.

The men that earn these large wages do not as a rule keep their money. They stop work in the winter, and spend what they have made, so that when summer comes round they have to resume their toilsome occupation, and hope for the coming of some gold discovery in which they can take a hand. The teams they drive are unlike those used in less mountainous regions. The waggons are large, heavy, high-boxed vehicles, fitted with heavy double breaks, having powerful leverage, without which the descent of the mountain slopes would be impossible, or rather so easy that no one would care about doing it. To make a team two of these waggons are fastened together, and from ten to sixteen animals, according to circumstance, harnessed to them. One man attends to the break on each waggon, and usually another drives. When horses or mules are harnessed in, the driver frequently rides the near wheeler, holding reins attached only to the leading horses. With one hand he guides these along the road, and with the other holds the strap with which he works the break lever. All day long he travels up and down the mountain sides, occasionally throwing a stone at his leaders who are beyond' the reach of his whip. At night he halts generally in the centre of the road, oftentimes in some narrow part where no other vehicle can pass without considerable trouble.

The bull-whackers camp early, turn their animals loose, cook their supper, and go to bed. As soon as the first streak of dawn appears, sometimes before it, they are up and out searching for their oxen. Several hours go by before the scattered animals are hunted up from bushes, hollows, and thickets, and then, breakfast being eaten, the whacker goes on his way again until the long shadows of the pines warn him that it is time to halt. They all hope, and believe, that when more people come in fresh discoveries will be made, and then the bull-whacking will be allowed " to rip" and the more alluring occupation of digging will be resumed. There is a weekly stage on this road, which is well horsed, well driven, and considering all things wonderfully safe. The nature of the road necessitates good and well-trained horses; such accidents as have happened were owing to scary horses. Of the road itself I will speak by-and-by. The stage fare to Cariboo is eighty dollars, and the same for returning, with a corresponding rate for intermediate places. This, with the four dollars a day for meals and bed (and one gentleman charged us a dollar and a half for luncheon and called me a "pompious gent" into the bargain, because I declined a cocktail with him), makes it difficult for poor men to travel on the road. The miner, going down flush in the fall, does not care very much what he pays; but the same individual returning in the spring, having spent in the pleasures of city life all that he had made by his toil in the mountains, is obliged to shoulder his pack and foot it along the weary miles until he strikes his destination and makes a pile, or comes out " dead broke."

While we were at Yale, an old mining hand came in from the mountains at the back of " Hope," where he had been prospecting. He had found a " crop out" (I think he called it) which would yield ninety-six dollars to the ton, and he spoke of this as being very good, because with that on the surface the vein beneath would be much richer. He said it was a difficult place to get at, and when he had recorded his claim, and other persons came to go in there, a good many of them would break their necks. He seemed to have found the place in an odd manner. While prospecting on the mountain, he and the Indian with him stopped to watch a grizzly bear that was chasing a mountain sheep. The sheep made for the craggy rock, jumping from one to the other, until he reached a place where nothing could follow him. Then he watched the bear with calm indifference, while that disappointed quadruped went off growling into a cave in the mountains. The miner then set off with the Indian lad to shoot the sheep, and had hardly gone twenty paces when a heavy avalanche of rock came down from the peak above, carrying away the place where he and the boy had been sitting; and in meandering partly to reach the sheep, and partly to find a new pass down the side, the fortunate prospector discovered the specimens which he showed us at Yale. He was going down to secure his claim by recording it: the rule being, as he said, that a discoverer was allowed a hundred feet, and if he chose to form a company of ten or more, then the grant might be made for five hundred feet, but that there the limit was.

It appears from everyone's account that now-a-days the mining camps and all interior places are orderly and tolerably free from crime. At the first start some well-known Californian rowdies came in, and for a while "ran the country;" but the English Government had appointed a Judge who took the bull by the horns, and asserted the supremacy of the law at once. A great many stories are told of Judge, now Sir Matthew, Begbie and the rowdies who came in with mining traditions of California, all having for their point the determination of the Judge that the law should be supreme. One story, as an example of many:—

A party of rowdies, on their road to the mines, were drinking in a way-side saloon. Judge Begbie, travelling up country, stopped at the house and entered the room where the miners were playing cards and drinking whiskey. He was recognized at once, and a leading spirit of the group commenced to enlarge upon the —— —— "bully" times he was going to have, and how he would run things in spite of the —— —— Britishers and their —— —— laws, winding up with some reference to —— —— judges, and a promise that the boys should see some —— —— shooting, every substantive being preceded by some ingeniously blasphemous oath.

This was intended as a brag for the Judge's edification, and to show him that he'd better be careful how he interfered with the speaker's little amusements; but the Judge, not seeing the thing in the right way, stepped across the room, tapped the gentleman on the shoulder, and remarked :—

"I've heard what you said, my friend, and I've only to add this, that whenever there is any shooting, I promise you there shall be some hanging after it."

As the astonished braggart looked up at the herculean form that stood over him, it may have occurred to him that if he said much more the vigorous individual who addressed him might not wait for the shooting, but might begin the hanging at once just to prevent unpleasantness. At any rate, the result of the manner in which the laws have been carried out in the interior of British Columbia is that, whereas at the first start the Indians murdered white men wherever they could safely do so, and Califordian rowdies threatened to make the place a hell, it soon came to be one of the safest and quietest places on the coast, and to-day there is no danger to be feared by a single wayfarer, rich or poor, than on the road between Hamilton and Toronto. There is not even a lawyer between Yale and Cariboo.

CHAPTER IV.

A Joke—Reported Dangers of the Road—A Privilege of English Nobility—Salmon Houses—Indian Method of Catching Salmon—Fish-drying Platforms—Cañons of the Fraser River—The Fraser—Hell Gate—A Dangerous-looking Road—The Rule of the Road—Courage of Lady Dufferin—Camp on Jackass Mountain.

AT Victoria we had been told that it was very doubtful whether horses could be found on the stage line to take us up country, owing to the fact of all extra accommodation being required for, and general arrangements having been disturbed by, the Vice-Regal party. But having telegraphed from New Westminster, mentioning our desire to get on, we received the cheering reply from a gentleman named Tingley, "All right; will govern ourselves accordingly." We found, on arrival, that while the only available coaches had been secured for the Governor-General and suite, Mr. Tingley, who is one of the partners in Barnard's stage line, and a gentleman who doesn't understand the word "impossible," had provided a double buggy and arranged relays of horses, as desired by telegram. He, himself, being the most experienced driver on the road, was to drive Lord and Lady Dufferin, though at one time this arrangement had nearly been upset by the facetiousness of his partner, Mr. Barnard. The latter came into the office where Mr. Tingley was sitting, and said :—

"Tingley, the Governor-General wants to bring his own carriages up, and we are to horse and drive them."

"Pshaw!" said Tingley. "They wouldn't last twenty miles on those hills, and they're not fitted with breaks."

"Well, he wants it, anyhow."

"All right. Bring them along, if he can stand it, I can."

"The aide-de-camp said," continued Barnard, "that the Earl would require the driver to wear his Lordship's livery."

Tingley took the cigar out of his mouth, looked at it without saying a word for a minute, and then asked,

"Well, and what did you say?"

"Well, I said I didn't quite know, I didn't think you'd be quite comfortable in them, specially if the knee-breeches was part of it, but that I knew you'd like to oblige his Lordship, so I wasn't sure but what you'd put them on all right."

"Oh, you said that, did you?" replied Tingley.

"Yes, but there's one point I didn't mention that the Earl's very particular about they say, and I didn't know how you might like it. You'll have to powder your hair."

"What did you say to that?" said Tingley.

"Well, I hesitated about it, but finally I said I guessed you'd come out in powder all right."

"Oh, you did, eh? You didn't mention that I'd like a bokay for my button-hole and a cocked-hat, did you?"

"No."

"Then I guess you had better drive that coach yourself."

The joke was then explained, and the services of the most energetic and courteous of stage-managers secured. We had heard a great deal in Victoria about the dangers and general appearance of this road, and I remembered having once read a rather alarming account of it in Milton and Cheedle's book. Moreover, we were told that when a certain eminent engineer—who some people say is a Scotchman, others a Canadian, and others a Fleming—went over the road, making a journey from one side of the continent to the other, he had insisted upon getting out to walk down the hills, so one felt little obliged to a gentleman who at Yale discussed the projected journey.

"You're one of the reporters, ain't yer?" he said.

We had at times been taken possession of as public property on the ground that we were reporters, so I thought I would draw the line.

"No, I'm not. I am a special correspondent."

He looked at me for a moment, then spat on the ground and said,

"Oh gosh!" then after a pause he added, "Are the others correspondents too?"

"Yes."

"Going in a double buggy, ain't yer?"

"Yes."

"All the accidents happens in buggies. Steve's accident happened in a buggy. First-rate driver is Steve—best on the line. Cornwall's accident—that's him as is a Senator down to Ottawa—happened in a buggy. Same double buggy as you're a-going up in. Steve—that's him as is going to drive the Earl—he got over the road and killed the horses and one passenger along of a wheelbarrow as the workmen had left on the road. It wasn't Steve's fault any."

"And how," I asked, "did Senator Cornwall come to grief?"

"Oh, he were driving with Captain Layton—that's him as is with the Earl's party now, with the white side whiskers and beard—going up with you again, I guess, ain't he?"

"Yes."

"Well, they were adriving the other side of Jackass Mountain, it happened when the nigh-side horse see a wheelbarrow in the road, and shied and pushed the other horse off the road. Luckily they didn't fall mor'n twenty feet, or they'd a-got hurt. Senator Cornwall he broke his leg."

"Are there any more accidents that you know of?" I asked.

"Why, you ain't skeared, are you?"

"No, I only asked."

"No, there ain't many accidents on this road. There was a double buggy backed off the road about a mile or so just round that first peak, killed a woman and a child, I guess, and here, right here by Spuzzum Creek, a mule-train got over. Killed two mules—didn't kill no drivers—they was on foot. But there never ain't any accidents worth speaking of on this road. I guess there ain't a better stage road going. There," he continued, pointing to Captain Layton, "that's him I was speaking of. Walks kinder lame, don't he?"

"Yes, the result of his accident with Senator Cornwall, I suppose?"

"Oh, no! it ain't. He didn't get no hurt. His leg got broke out of a double buggy agetting off the road some time ago. Wheelbarrow I guess, most times it's on account of wheelbarrows — men mending the road."

"Are there any men mending the road now?"

"Yes, a good many, I guess. Biggest freshet this spring we ever had—did a lot of damage, mor'n a hundred dollars, I guess. If you was to get into a accident they'd put a piece about it in your paper, I guess, wouldn't they?"

"Very likely," I said. "It wouldn't make a bad item."

"Might do harm to the road then if you was to get over. That would be bad. This yere's the Earl coming now, ain't it? Is that his Countess? She's mighty young, ain't she, for a Countess?"

I told him that it was a privilege of the nobility in England when their wives got old to take younger ones and give the title to them, and that the old ones were all called dowagers, but that this was the only wife Lord Dufferin had ever had, and that she was still a young woman. Then

I went off to see the buggy that had broken Senator Cornwall's leg, and in which we were to go to Kamloops, forming some mental resolutions as to what I would do when wheelbarrows loomed up on the road.

In order to keep ahead of the Governor-General, who travelled with four horses while we limited ourselves to two, and witness his arrival at each point, we started early next morning, and drove for some way along the bank of the river, the driver indicating the place where the mule team had "got over" and killed the mules, and the spot where the most recent fatal buggy accident had taken place. We had not gone more than a mile or two when we saw a wheelbarrow which some idiot had left on the mountain-side of the road, in defiance of the rule which prescribes that everything should be left on the outer side, and a little way beyond it an old Indian woman, ugly enough to frighten any number of horses, standing staring at us from a projecting point of stone on the mountain-side. We passed these waifs satisfactorily, and then drove on at a brisk rate along an excellent road which gradually ascended the side of the heights along which we were travelling. Our attention was attracted at once by curious looking dog-kennel-like structures, high up in the pine-trees along the road, beneath each of which the trunk of the tree, was encircled by a band of tin, one edge of which was made to fit closely on the tree while the other projected outwards, making a mushroom shape round the trunk. The structures above looked like Indian graves, which are sometimes placed up amongst the branches; but they proved to be "salmon houses," in which the dried fish is stored for the winter, the tin attachment preventing martens and other vermin from climbing and stealing. The Indians of the Fraser River live almost exclusively on fish, and during the season when the salmon are running up the river to their spawning places the great take is looked for. All along the river in its narrower parts, and particularly in the cañons, the scaffoldings, hand nets, and drying places of the Indians can be seen. The road passes so much of the river at a considerable, though varying, elevation, that the Indians fishing look like pigmies, and the Fraser, of whose terrors we have heard so much, presents, at least when seen from a little height, only one or two places where a well-manned canoe would hesitate to run.

In olden days, before the traffic begotten of the mines furnished them with packwork, the salmon was the main stay of the Indians. The more common way of catching the fish is by means of a small net, in shape like a jelly bag, fastened to the end of a long pole having an oval termination to fit the mouth of the net. The Indian, taking his stand on a projecting rock or platform which he has rigged for himself, dips his net into the water where an eddy working up stream keeps the back of the net in the same direction. Sometimes he scoops with the net, drawing it down the stream; sometimes allows it to remain stationary. When a fish enters the net the fact at once becomes apparent, and the Indian raises his net, oftentimes, when the salmon is large, with considerable difficulty, and then, before attempting to take his prey out of the trap, hits him on the head with a hatchet, and lands him on the rocks. His klootchmen (squaw) then takes the salmon in hand, and in a few minutes it is stretched out over the edifice of poles upon which the drying takes place. We saw several caught as we passed along, high up above the fishermen, and all in this manner.

Lord Dufferin descended the hill at one place and went out upon a fisherman's platform, but found that it was exceedingly wobbley and insecure, and came to the conclusion that the rush of a large salmon would have proved fatal. In all the collections of Indian huts along the road, there were several fish-drying scaffoldings covered with salmon, and some of the houses which we entered were so very salmony that it became necessary, after the first few moments, to rush for the fresh air. This diet has the peculiar effect of wearing away the teeth of the Indians, so that you constantly see comparatively young people with the smallest possible remains of dental force.

After travelling for about twelve miles up the left bank of the Fraser, the road crosses the river over a suspension bridge and ascends the hill on the other side. In the first day's journey the principal cañons of the Fraser come into view, and the most rapid part of the river—at least, on this side of the Kamloops journey—is reached. The mountains at these points approach one another very closely, and at one time met amongst the rocks which

THE FRASER RIVER. 119

now overhang the river. The Fraser, a yellow, muddy-looking stream of very inconsiderable width, comes down from the mountains with great force, and cuts its way along the valleys between the several divisions of the Cascade range. At some points it narrows and works itself up into a series of continuous rapids, and at other places opens out a little and flows along more evenly. Looking upon it from above, one invests it with the attributes of a living creature. Its angry rush and its calmer progression, as it meets and then passes the obstructions the mountains have hurled at its bosom, seem to be in keeping only with a being of life. It has come along for many weary miles in spite of all that has been done to impede it, cutting its way here, and washing away that which would have hindered it elsewhere, until towards its place of final rest it meets the solid rock upon which its close embracing foes have rested through the ages. The result one can imagine to have been a fearful struggle, in which the river again achieved the victory by seizing upon its enemy and wrenching it apart, and to the present day the victorious river roars out an angry defiance as it rushes past the torn, jagged, and unanswering foe that would have barred its way, and which is now doomed for ages to stand as a monument of its own defeat. We know, of course, that time was the ally that helped the Fraser in its fight, but the cañons give the impression of having been torn, not worn, into a pathway for the river.

At a place called "Hell Gate," the road-makers had constructed a railed platform on the overhanging rock, in order that the Governor-General might see the cañon from its narrowest and most interesting point. We saw here that my friend at Yale had been justified in speaking of the freshet as the biggest he had known. The river was at least seventy feet below us, while twenty feet above the road were the high water marks of the spring freshet, so that there was a difference of ninety feet visible to us, though one gentleman told us it had been over a hundred. At this point also they have thought it well to place a low outer wall on the precipice edge of the road, for there is a sharp turn and a rapid descent, where any mistake on the part of the animals would be fatal. I may say at once with regard to this road that it looks, and when spoken about appears to be, much more dangerous than it really is. To gallop down an incline high up on the side of a precipitous mountain, with the Fraser roaring five or six hundred feet beneath you, and sometimes scarcely a foot between the outer wheel and eternity, does not sound to be essentially a comfortable operation, but there is no more danger of going off the road than there would be in driving along a prairie road. If you do happen to go in a bad place the result depends, as the Lewiston brakeman said, very much upon how you have behaved yourself in this world, but practically speaking very few people do go.

The stage line has been running for seventeen years, and no stage has ever yet gone over. The stages are, of course, well horsed, care being taken that the leaders, upon whom so much depends, are not skittish, scary animals, and the coaches are fitted with powerful breaks, so that if the leaders went, it would be within possibility to hold up the wheelers and stage until the others had been cut adrift. This has happened in the case of freight teams, the drivers of which are frequently struggling through the effects of a previous night's debauch. The most awkward moments are in passing a heavily laden waggon-team. The rule of the road is that the lighter teams go outside. Taking our own case as an example, it happened that we had to pass a team of sixteen oxen at a very narrow, crumbly part of the road. There was just room to go by, provided we could push one ox closer into his chain, and the driver went at him for this purpose. We did succeed in successfully crowding him, but he resented the assault, and turning his heels towards us let drive at the inside horse. He was, fortunately, a little late, but had he reached his object, the animal might, and probably would, have started from him, and pushed the outer horse over the side. We all concluded that for the future, when it was necessary to crowd in on the oxen to get by, we would get out and see how it was done. It is nervous work also on first galloping down a hill where the road turns sharply round a spur of the mountains. It appears to one that the slightest irregularity will send the carriage over the precipice, and that, so far as any one can see, the horses are galloping straight over, for the road appears to lead up to the edge of a precipice and there stop. It is not until you arrive at the very point of the spur that the wind of the road becomes visible. With six horses, with which the stage is sometimes driven, the two leaders have gone out of sight—heaven knows where —before the passengers can discover any route on which to continue their wild career. There was such a place during the first day's drive, and on reaching the other end, we almost simultaneously expressed the hope that Lady Dufferin would not be frightened (I believe we all were), so in the evening, when opportunity offered, I asked Mr. Tingley, who had himself driven Lord and Lady Dufferin's team, how his passengers got on.

"They got on bully," he said.

"Was Lady Dufferin frightened?" I asked.

"Didn't scare worth a cent. There isn't a scare in her. She's better than any of 'em; jumps out fast to walk up the big hills, and I pick her last of any of 'em. She's first-rate. You can't find any-one to beat her."

Lady Dufferin wins and certainly merits the highest encomiums from all who travel with her; but on comparing notes, it appeared that she, too, had misgivings about bullock trains, and, unlike some others, honestly confessed it. But all nervous feelings about the road wear off, and on the second journey the appearance of a team, or train, of pack mules alone caused any thought about the road.

A camp had been pitched for the Governor-General about forty-five miles up the road on a height called Jackass Mountain, and here Lord and Lady Dufferin rested on the first evening. We walked up to the camp to pay a visit to Her Excellency at the Government House-under-canvas, and found that some one, I believe Mr. Dewdney, had arranged a most complete little retreat on a spur of the mountain commanding a magnificent view of the cañon. Sometimes, as on the return journey, this cañon is filled with a thick heavy bank of fog, held in by the two mountains, and lying low down upon the river. From Jackass Mountain you look down upon it, and see this thick table-like mass of white cloud slowly surging against the confining rocks below you—when you throw a stone into it you wonder whether it will stick in the middle or get through. And stone-throwing from the heights above the Fraser has a fascination about it which is not to be resisted, and is only excelled by the kindred amusement of rolling boulders down the mountain side. I saw a correspondent, a staid and serious man of letters, with the evidence of intellectual pursuits in the scantiness of his hair and the strength of his spectacles, grow energetic, excited and warm in the occupation of racing boulders into the "Thompson." I heard another correspondent, whose erudition and comprehensive grasp of great topics made his society enchanting, suddenly consign the contending parties in the United States, of whose chances he was enlightening us, to everlasting oblivion at the sight of a really good boulder, and the " Globe" correspondent, forgetting, for a moment, the dignity that should appertain to representatives of that journal, and resenting some allusions to future obesity, joined in the amusement and succeeded in winning the admiration of his companions by his deftness in an art which he had acquired, in spite of the painsgiving protests of his early preceptors. Even the most inner circle of the vice-regal party admitted in tones of deep regret that they had been interrupted in the entrancing pastime referred to, by the exigencies of the journey; and it is beyond doubt that were the two Houses of Parliament to be placed in a given spot a match would forthwith be made between the Speakers thereof, and that the Members would wager hats and champagne on the result, so volatile do the gravest become under this influence.

CHAPTER V.

Lytton—Reception of the Governor-General—Indian Gala Day—Indian Villages and Houses—Indian Graves—Lax Morality of Indian Belles—The Thompson River—Cook's Ferry, or Spence's Bridge—A Modest Indian Maiden—Bunch Grass—Trout-fishing —Arrival at Kamloops—A Master of Etiquette— Flogging of Indian Women.

FIFTY-SEVEN miles from Yale, and early in the second day's travel, is the small mining town of Lytton. In the old days of the gold excitement in its neighbourhood, it was a lively and flourishing little town, but its customers have passed on, and it is now comparatively deserted, remote, and melancholy slow. Nevertheless, it displayed the remains of former energies in the manner and spirit of receiving the Governor-General. The principal, or, at least, the most novel feature of this reception was the assemblage of Indians who had come together at the English mission, situated about a mile before the town is reached. An arch had been erected over the road opposite to the church door, and bodies of mounted Indians, men and women, headed by their spiritual guide—the Rev. Mr. Good—stood ready to receive the representative of Her Majesty. When they had expressed their sentiments of loyalty to the Crown and the Dominion, a cavalcade was formed, of which the foremost part was composed of mounted men, and that portion which came after the carriages of women. The women were dressed in their best and gayest garments, flaming petticoats, and a bright coloured handkerchief bound round the head of each. They rode astride their horses, like the Kanaka girls of the Sandwich Islands, and carried their children either behind them on the saddle or in an Indian cradle before them. Sometimes two girls shared one horse, and came galloping along, laughing and kicking, but in the majority of cases each had her own steed.

A large number of the animals ridden were mares, and every mare was followed by a colt. The party had come from the mission at a rapid rate, the Indians galloping in front and in rear, and whipping their horses to keep in proper order, so that when the Governor-General arrived at the main arch all the colts were astray and whinnying for their dams, and all their anxious mothers whinnying in return, which, with the hallooing of the Indians themselves and the voices of the white people of the town, created a hub-bub in which it was impossible to hear or to be heard. It was a great gala day for these Indians, and they all appeared to be enjoying themselves to the utmost, with the exception of one or two unfortunate urchins who had been bound to their respective mothers with shawls in such a way that while their bodies were held fast, their tiny heads rolled round and wagged about so furiously that when the cavalcade had passed on one looked round to see if any heads had been left behind. These Indians—once called, from their anamosity to, and dealings with, white men "The Knife Indians"—are now a peaceable tribe of useful mountaineers. They all possess horses, which they have raised or purchased from the white settlers. They never walk unless all their animals are employed packing, and they seem to be rapidly adopting the customs of their white neighbours.

At several points along the road we came upon their villages, the houses of which were built in more or less rude imitation of civilized dwellings, and their gardens showed considerable labour and care. In the winter, however, they abandon these houses and live, several families together, in a dwelling peculiar to themselves. This is very primitive, very warm, and very dirty. The house is built in this way—a large circular hole about four feet in depth and perhaps forty feet in circumference is dug. Four upright posts are placed in this, making as large a square as possible, and rafters laid across. A roof of poles is then laid from the edge of the circle, and this is covered with bark and thickly overlaid with earth all round. Egress and ingress are made up and down a notched spar protruding through an aperture in the roof which performs the treble duty of window, door, and chimney. Viewed from the outside, this winter residence might be taken for the dwelling of a large species of burrowing animal, which, by the way, is exactly what its inhabitants are for the time being. But as spring comes round they leave these retreats, when it is found that so very large a number of uninvited and troublesome guests have taken refuge in the house itself as well as in the clothing and bedding of the residents, that the house is not usually occupied a second winter, a new one being built for the coming season.

In many places we came across the graves of deceased Indians. The bodies in these were buried beneath the ground —a method of burial not always adopted by the Indians. One sepulchre which we examined contained three graves—I think of two men and one woman. The bodies had been placed side by side, and the grave, not covered with earth, but roofed over with boards. A lean-to shed had been built over these combined graves, with the sides completely and the front partially shut in. In front of the shed, just inside its posts, was the family canoe broken into three parts, and there were three copper boiling-pots inverted, one on each grave. Outside the shed the ordinary cooking utensils of the dead persons were tied to the poles, and two many-studded guns, rusted and decaying from exposure, swung from a sappling which, bending beneath their weight, drooped over the last resting-place of these mountain wanderers. The basket in which the woman had carried berries from the wood or fish from the mountain streams was fastened above her grave; the dark green blankets which had covered the Indians in life now fluttered in the wind, weird-looking ensigns, waiting to be claimed by the spirits of their departed owners. On a large branch of the nearest tree hung the heads, hides, and hoofs of the horses which had carried the deceased persons in life, and furnished the funeral baked-meats on their departure to the land of the hereafter. Immediately in front of the shed were placed three wooden figures, carved to represent the honoured dead, and clothed in garments which their prototypes would have deemed the acme of self-adornment.

"Rank grows the grass, the willows ghostly wave,
O'er the last wigwam of the Indian brave,"

sings a friend of mine; but the poor savage does what in him lies to mark the resting place of his relatives, and at least refrains from grabbing at the personal property which may be left behind. Now a rich uncle's death, according to our system of thought, is——

I fear that the Indians of this road are in most cases a little lax in respect of certain points in the decalogue. The miners and others have a demoralizing effect upon the savage belle. All those bright coloured garments that we saw— Alas! the temptation to outdress their sisters is as irresistible there as in the cities of the east, and the shelves of the trader's store is the same prolific cause of ruin as the windows of an eastern dry-goods store. Whiskey and dry-goods have the same obliterating and amalgamating effects here as elsewhere. The missionary at Lytton rode by us and explained —good easy man—that the contact of the whites and Indians was beneficial to the latter. They dressed better since civilization had come amongst them, followed the manners and customs of the white men more than before, and even, he said, became more like them in personal appearance. He thought this was a great step gained, and believed it to have been all done by some immaterial agency to the influence of which Indian savagery succumbed rapidly and unfailingly. The idea entertained by the residents of Lytton and other places as to cause and effect was not exactly in harmony with the parson's theory.

At Lytton the Thompson, with its clear green water, falls into the muddy Fraser, and runs along the channel of that river for nearly a mile before consenting to amalgamate with its dirtier sister. I suppose that the Fraser looks dirtier than it really is, for one never heard of salmon running up a stream so muddy as the Fraser appears to be. At this point the road to Kamloops leaves the Fraser altogether, and continues along the Thompson, the characterisitics of the country being, for a short distance, much the same as before. On the second day out we crossed the Thompson over a somewhat shaky bridge, at a place called indifferently " Cook's Ferry," or " Spence's Bridge," where a most elaborate mid-day meal had been provided. The proprietor of this hostelrie, though having no conscience in the matter of charging, certainly possessed an exceptionally clever culinary " John"—all the cooks are Chinamen—and we shared an excellent luncheon—one which an American would certainly have called " a real elegant lunch"—with all the house flies that could conveniently assemble for the feast. The flies along the road had heard of this luncheon, and had left the other places, even before our arrival, to meet at Spence's Bridge, and very quietly but firmly took possession of certain wondrous-looking structures that were on the table or the sideboard, leaving us the more substantial viands. Soon after leaving Lytton we passed through the last of the Cascade range proper, and on leaving Spence's Bridge, began to strike the Bunch-Grass county.

As evening closed in we were driving over level country, with hills, not mountains, rising at varying distances on either side of us. Going up to Kamloops we had little opportunity of seeing this, because rain was falling heavily and the hour was late. It was raining slightly when we left Yale, and we were confidently told that when we had driven a few hours and were well up in the mountains the rain would cease; but, nevertheless, it rained all day. At night the indefatigable controller of the road told me that he hoped it would be fine to-morrow. "It don't rain," he said, "three days in the year here. I don't give a continental—something—for myself, but it would beat H—l if it should rain just when she's going up." He was thinking of Lady Dufferin. It did rain pretty steadily next day, but not in sufficient quantities to have any effect on the place he mentioned. But it was raining hard and the night was pitch black when we arrived at the inn at Ashcroft. This is Senator Cornwall's estate.

The Governor-General and Lady Dufferin stayed for the night at Mr. Cornwall's private residence, although their host, from having driven over the cliff, was nursing a broken leg elsewhere. The inn was crammed full when we arrived, and the landlord was much excited about the coming of this buggy full of wet travellers, and suggested that we should drive to Cache Creek, six miles further on, where he said we should find comfortable quarters and be able to get our things dried. But one of the correspondents commended him to the society of a person where he would have very quickly been dried himself, and flatly declined to go any further. Here, also, we found an excellent "John" in possession of the kitchen, and after dinner, the night having cleared up, we drove on to Cache Creek. We were rewarded for this by obtaining a comfortable bed instead of a blanket on the floor, or in the hay loft, and more liberal washing arrangements in the morning than had been quite usual. Moreover, before starting, we witnessed the assembling of another mounted cavalcade of Indians, men and women, who were about to proceed to Ashcroft to escort the Governor-General down to Cache Creek.

Here the writer of this unwillingly disturbed the serenity of an Indian maiden. I had walked to the other side of the cavalcade of women, and was quietly watching the general proceedings, without paying special attention to anyone in particular, when I observed a native beauty not yet mounted, who had been struggling with her horse to place him in such a position near the rock that she could get upon his back. Her companions were calling upon her to come on, and she stood looking from them to me, at first in good-humour, but gradually becoming annoyed. I offered to assist her, but that was evidently not what she wanted, for she jabbered at me snappishly. Still her companions shouted and still she hesitated, and her horse, growing impatient, began to back away from the advantageous position in which she had placed him. Then I approached her a second time, but she grew very angry and voluble, evidently endeavouring to impress something upon my understanding which her language of course failed to reach. At last, with the assistance of a grinning young Indian, I discovered that she wished to mount her horse—of course, astride, after the fashion of her countrywomen, and did not like my standing close on the off side of the animal. Cheered by the evidence of a modesty which I had not dreamt of, and certainly never intended to offend, I walked off leaving the dusky Diana to mount in peace.

From this point we observed the great change in the nature of the country that had commenced even before dusk of the previous day. The hills formed benches or small table-lands at various heights and of varying dimensions along either side of the road, and, of course, beyond the limits of our view. These hills were covered with wormwood and here and there a little sage. A large part of this district is covered with bunch-grass, a very nutritious kind of feed, but in the immediate neighbourhood of the road we did not see any. Where the bunch-grass has been eaten down, repeatedly wormwood springs up and answers the purpose of the plant it has displaced. One or two owners of cattle told me that stock prefer this wormwood, and that it is better for them for winter feed.

The valleys along the Thompson, varying from half a mile to a mile and a quarter in width, are well farmed, but the farms are all cultivated by means of irrigation.

The farmers do not complain of this necessity, for though it involves some trouble and a little additional expense at starting, there is the certainty of reaping a good crop, a result which in places watered only by the rainfall is sometimes doubtful. The crops taken this year from one or two of the ranches which we passed, averaged forty bushels to the acre. But stock-raising is the principal operation here undertaken. There is not sufficient market for extensive grain raising, and the country is well adapted for feeding cattle. Throughout the summer large bands of cattle feed in the mountain range, the hilly bunch-grass country to the east of the range being kept for winter grazing. The winds clear the tops and upper sides of the hills, so that the animals find both food and shelter, and in spite of the thermometer ranging far below zero are enabled to winter out and grow fat. And bunch-grass fed beef and mutton are things of themselves. Other beef may be good, but it is not bunch-grass beef. A four-year-old Southdown is a thing of beauty and a joy for ever-so-long as he lasts, but if the downs of Sussex and Hampshire were clad with bunch-grass, the native Southdown would be reserved for the tables of emperors. In vain do the Vancouver Islanders pine for this succulent food. It must be eaten in the mountains or not at all, for let an ox be ever so fat he will on the journey down the mountains lose flesh and fat, and grumblingly eat, if he will eat at all, such food as may be given in lieu of his native bunch-grass. A certain traveller, in speaking of his arrival at Kamloops from across the Rocky Mountains, tells us how he ate almost continuously for three days, and we understood his difficulty in leaving off.

Bunch-grass became an adjective in the Governor-General's party, and any person with whom one was very much pleased was described as a "bunch-grass good fellow," and trout of a superior quality as regular bunch-grass fish. Some of these were caught by Lady Dufferin. In fact no one else caught anything except a correspondent, who hooked a very fine snag. But Lady Dufferin is an expert sportswoman and throws a fly faultlessly. To her belongs the undivided honour of having beguiled the wily trout of Thompson River. At Savona's Ferry the Thompson River flows out of Kamloops Lake, and is thence called the Lower Thompson, in contradistinction to the Upper Thompson, which flows into the lake at the other end, where the Hudson's Bay Post, village, and R. C. Mission of Kamloops is situated. At the head of the Lower Thompson Lady Dufferin went ashore and searched about for a likely spot for trout. The proprietor of the ferry was ready with the universal comforting intelligence that her ladyship ought to have been there yesterday. To-day there was too much wind, but yesterday she would without fail have found sport. Two days before when going up the lake, the same person said to the fishing correspondent, "Ah! You ought to have been here last week. It's too hot to-day, but last week they rose to the fly well."

A traveller in this country may take it for granted that the season in which he is travelling is an unusual one; never rained there before his arrival; the summer is hotter than ever was known before, or the inhabitants never remembered such a winter; the day on which he tries to fish is too windy or too bright; the birds when he goes shooting will be found to have left the district suddenly and without reason, and he is confidently told that if he had arrived last week there was plenty of game, and that deer were seen right within shot of the house, or that if he will only wait a week or ten days he will be sure to have good sport. In spite, however, of the usual mistiming of arrival, Lady Dufferin began by striking two fish, one on each fly, and after playing them through the rapid in a—may I say " masterly ?"—

manner, landed both of them, and followed up her first success by killing several others. Colonel Littleton, too, in spite of the fact that he ought to have been there last week to find prairie chickens, killed five brace, and as fish and grouse were all obtained in the space of an hour or two, the general result was not so much to be complained of.

Here at the ferry we left the road—which we might have continued round the lake—and saw for the present the last of the irritating bullock-teams and erratic pack trains. We had all more or less conceived a dislike of these useful institutions, for the latter with their protruding packs ruthlessly crowded us on to the edge of the precipice whenever we met them, and the former by camping exactly in the middle of the road not only caused us trouble and difficulty, but took it ill that anyone should travel on the high road after they had camped. We embarked on board a steamer at Savona's

RECEPTION AT KAMLOOPS. 149

Ferry, and started for Kamloops, twenty-five miles up the lake and two hundred and fifty-eight miles from New Westminster. This boat, belonging to Mr. Mara (a Canadian) and others, was built by the Hudson's Bay Company during the mining excitement, but not proving a great success was sold. She is the only boat on the lake, and I do not think that at present there is much inducement to build another. We arrived at Kamloops in the afternoon of Saturday, the 9th, and the Governor-General landed and was escorted by a large mounted cavalcade of white men and Indians through the town.

On the day of our arrival at Kamloops, the Governor-General and Lady Dufferin went on shore, where they were received by a cavalcade composed of the gentlemen of the place and a gathering of Indian horsemen, who were divided into three bands, each led by a chief carrying an English ensign. There was a deal of galloping about and general manœuvring amongst the Indians, and we obtained from looking at them some idea of how effective they might be on the plains as irregular cavalry when properly handled. "Sitting Bull," however, has given a melancholy proof that when well generaled they can be very effective.

At Kamloops the Governor-General was received with the usual cordial expressions of good will, welcome, and loyalty that have been observable elsewhere in this Province, and Lady Dufferin was presented with a bouquet by a lady who had performed a similar act at Claneboye on the day of her ladyship's marriage. This reception at Kamloops was the occasion of a somewhat amusing occurrence. In the village was the son of an English gentleman of position, once head-master of one of our greatest public schools. The population generally appeared to call him "Hennesy," that being a name well known in the mountains, and phonetically resembling the one properly appertaining to the gentleman in question. The Kamloops representative of the family is one of those who divide the seasons into a time for work and a time for that bibulous ecstasy which even Roman Emperors thought worthy of cultivation and garlands of roses. When it was known that Lord Dufferin was coming to Kamloops, the possession of a real gentleman who knew all about lords and the way of receiving them, and whose public school teaching would now come into play, if never before, was a subject of congratulation. Kamloops had in its neighbourhood such a one, and he was coming to teach the rough idea of the mountains how to shoot compliments at a vice-regal couple. He came, and—as my informant told me—spent seventy dollars in a suit of clothes for the occasion. He assisted in coaching those who desired to learn the art of addressing a Governor-General and his consort, and everything bid fair to harvest for the sustainer of good old English courtesy an abundant crop of undying laurels.

Alas! such is the mutability of human affairs, this master of etiquette, perhaps remembering the saying which ascribes intoxication to the nobility, and thinking that he, too, should get "as drunk as a Lord" in order to receive an Earl properly, or perhaps suffering from thirst caused by the heat of the arguments into which he was obliged to enter, was found, when the moment of the anticipated triumph arrived, to be in a state of hallucination as to the order of the intended proceedings and his own position therein, and to have suddenly cast to the winds the deferential regard for viceregal authority and familiarity with good manners which had combined to raise him so high above his fellows. He had instead conceived an idea that the voice of Kamloops was to determine the course of the Pacific Railway, and that Kamloops was at the moment overawed, and under this hallucination he had blossomed forth as a tribune of the people in the noisy stage of intoxication. The population could not have been more astonished had they been suddenly called upon to hear the Usher of the Black Rod rise from his seat to denounce the existence of an Upper Chamber. He was called to bless, and lo! he got drunk and cursed, and seemed inclined to continue cursing. However, two of his friends took him in charge, one interrupting his remarks by the simple but effectual mode of literally shutting his mouth, while both took him by the arms and led him off. They were very tender and cajoling with him while in the immediate neighbourhood of Lord and Lady Dufferin, but so soon as they had cleared the corner of the arch their manner changed and they hustled him off with kicks and curses, calling him in some language with metaphor rich the son of some four-legged animal which—as Mr. Barham says—it is not necessary here to mention. It was the fall of a great man at the moment when the world was to look on and admire. Kamloops, however, did very well without him, and presented the Governor-General with a very loyal and cordial address, to which he replied with the same happiness of expression which characterizes all his speeches.

At Kamloops one gained a better idea of the country beyond the Cascade range than it had been easy to acquire before. It is surrounded by bunch-grass country, which extends for a great distance in every direction. Vast herds can be grazed here and wintered without care or housing. Horses are numerous. All people, including the Indians, ride, and would refuse to walk. As we came up the lake a band of horses, numbering three hundred or more, belonging to the Hudson's Bay Company, came rushing out of a wood to water at the river, and at the Indian village we saw numbers of horses of all ages and sizes. The Governor-General went over on the day after his reception at Kamloops to see the Indians at this mission, where he met the principal men and conversed with them. This mission, doubtless, does some good amongst the Indians—probably a great deal of good—but there are some objectionable features about it. A provincial dignitary of considerable altitude —I mean in position—was inclined to take me to task for discussing the question of the discipline enforced at this mission. It appeared, according to what I had learnt from those I took to be trustworthy authorities, that not only was the discipline of the Church exceedingly severe, such penance being enforced upon the Indians as no other people in the Roman Catholic world would submit to, but that for certain offences the Indian women were flogged.

The assertion on the Kamloops side was that this flogging was done by the chief on the priest's order. This allegation, I was told by the objecting dignitary, was nonsense. But the flogging was not denied, the only answer to it being that we flogged women a hundred years ago in Bridewell, a reply which did not happen to convince me of its propriety. The flogging, it was urged, might be done without the priests discountenancing it, but it was done by the chief according to some tribal usage. It will occur to most people who are acquainted with missions among the Indians, that no such institution exists or could for one week exist contrary to the wish of the priest, nor, under the circumstance of every other white man in the neighbourhood denouncing it, without some very decided countenance being given it by him. I was quite satisfied in my own mind, from what I had heard, that the priest was virtually the *sub-rosâ* inflictor of the punishment, but I subsequently made inquiries from other persons than those I had asked, one of whom was himself "a dignitary," and I quoted the adverse opinion. The reply was that it was "bosh;" that the flogging of the women at Kamloops was done, if not by the direct order of the priest, at least with such connivance on his part as amounted to the same thing, and that at some other mission, the name of which I forget, the same thing is done.

The cover for this transaction is "tribal rule," but if the English law has superseded tribal law, and if we do not permit one Indian to kill another, or burn his house, or destroy his goods, even though it may be permitted or required by "tribal law," it is not very easy to understand why we are to stop short and permit a barbarous punishment to be perpetrated under the cloak of "tribal law," which has been condemned by every English-speaking community throughout the world. The infliction of this punishment at Kamloops, on the showing of the gentleman who seemed to defend it—for whose person and office I desire to express my profoundest respect—has not even the merit of being impartial. A woman is flogged for an offence to which she has been persuaded by a person whom neither priest nor Indian chief dare lay hands upon. The fault is committed oftentimes through the influence of whiskey, and the weaker and least guilty party is seized upon and brutally punished while her partner remains inviolate. It was with some reluctance that assent was given by public opinion to the proposition that the most brutal roughs of the back slums in our cities should be liable to corporal punishment, and those who think that the day is past for applying the lash to the back of a woman will not modify their opinion in the event of that punishment being applied by the virtual order of an irresponsible and self-constituted authority, and under circumstances that render its infliction a gross piece of injustice. Still less will they be satisfied when they remember that the silent mentor by whose wish the thing is done, belongs to a class which to-day are found, and for centuries have shown themselves, unfit to be trusted with the power of awarding secular penalties. If offences against morals are to be punished as offences against law, then we may ask that what is crime in a woman may be made crime in a man, and that the power that issues sentence shall be a responsible one; that some understanding shall be had as to the extent to which spiritual offences are to be considered legal offences; and that the punishment shall be one that civilized men may approve, and not one exhumed from the buried codes of savage law.

CHAPTER VI.

Speech of the Governor-General at Victoria.

BEFORE leaving for his northward trip, the Governor-General intimated that on his return he would meet those gentlemen who had formed the various Reception Committees, and communicate to them an expression of opinion upon the subject of the country and its relationship to the Dominion. From this arose the general impression that he was going to say something about the railway, though no one could exactly determine in his own mind to what extent Lord Dufferin would feel himself at liberty to carry his remarks. It was with very close attention, therefore that the following speech was heard when the Governor General met the Commitees at Government House this morning :—

Gentlemen,

I am, indeed, very glad to have an opportunity before quitting British Columbia of thanking you, and through you the citizens of Victoria, not only for the general kindness and courtesy I have met with during my residence amongst you, but especially for the invitation to the banquet with which you have honoured me. I regret extremely that my engagements did not permit me to accept this additional proof of your hospitality, but my desire to see as much as possible of the country and my other engagements forced me most reluctantly to decline it. I shall, however, have a final opportunity of mingling with your citizens at the entertainment arranged for me at Beacon Hill this afternoon, to which I am looking forward with the greatest pleasure. Perhaps, gentlemen, I may be also permitted to take advantage of this occasion to express to you the satisfaction and enjoyment I have derived from my recent progress through such portions of the Province as I have been able to reach within the short period left at my disposal.

I am well aware that I have visited but a small proportion of your domains, and that there are important centres of population from which I have been kept aloof. More especially have I to regret my inability to reach Cariboo, the chief theatre of your mining industry and the home of a community with whose feelings, wishes and sentiments it would have been very advantageous for me to have become personally acquainted. Still by dint of considerable exertion I have traversed the entire coast of British Columbia from its southern extremity to Alaska. I have penetrated to the head of Bute Inlet, I have examined the Seymour Narrows, and the other channels which intervene between the head of Bute Inlet and Vancouver Island. I have looked into the mouth of Dean's Canal and passed across the entrance to Gardner's Channel. I have visited Mr. Duncan's wonderful settlement at Metlakatlah, and the interesting Methodist mission at Fort Simpson, and have thus been enabled to realize what scenes of primitive peace and innocence, of idyllic beauty and material comfort, can be presented by the stalwart men and comely maidens of an Indian community under the wise administration of a judicious and devoted Christian missionary. I have passed across the intervening Sound of Queen Charlotte's Island to Skidegate, and studied with wonder the strange characteristics of a Hydah village with its forest of heraldic pillars. I have been presented with a sinister opportunity of descending upon a tribe of our Pagan savages in the very midst of their drunken orgies and barbarous rites, and after various other explorations I have had the privilege of visiting under very gratifying circumstances the Royal City of New Westminster.

Taking from that spot a new departure, we proceeded up the valley of the Fraser, where the river has cloven its way through the granite ridges and bulwarks of the Cascade range, and along a road of such admirable construction, considering the engineering difficulties of the line and the modest resources of the colony when it was built, as does the greatest credit to the able administrator who directed its execution. Passing thence into the open valleys and rounded eminences beyond, we had an opportunity of appreciating the pastoral resources and agricultural capabilities of what is known as the bunch-grass country. It is needless to say that wherever we went we found the same kindness, the same loyalty, the same honest pride in their country and its institutions which characterize the English race throughout the world, while Her Majesty's Indian subjects on their spirited horses, which the ladies of their families seemed to bestride with as much ease and grace as their husbands and brothers, notwithstanding the embarrassment of one baby on the pommel and another on the crupper, met us everywhere in large numbers and testified in their untutored fashion their genuine loyalty and devotion to their White Mother.

Having journeyed into the interior as far as Kamloops, and admired from a lofty eminence in its neighbourhood what seemed an almost interminable prospect of grazing lands and valleys susceptible of cultivation, we were forced with much reluctance to turn our face homewards to Victoria. And now that I am back it may, perhaps, interest you to learn what are the impressions I have derived during my journey. Well, I may frankly tell you that I think British Columbia a glorious Province—a Province which Canada should be proud to possess, and whose association with the Dominion she ought to regard as the crowning triumph of Federation. Such a spectacle as its coast line presents is not to be paralleled by any country in the world. Day after day for a whole week, in a vessel of nearly two thousand tons, we threaded an interminable labyrinth of watery lanes, and reaches that wound endlessly in and out of a network of islands, promontories and peninsulas for thousands of miles unruffled by the slightest swell from the adjoining ocean, and presenting at every turn an ever shifting combination of rock, verdure, glacier, and snow-capped mountain of unrivalled grandeur and beauty.

When it is remembered that this wonderful system of navigation, equally well adapted to the largest line of battle-ship and the frailest canoe, fringes the entire sea-board of your Province and communicates at points sometimes more than a hundred miles from the coast, with a multitude of valleys stretching eastward into the interior, at the same time that it is furnished with innumerable harbours on either hand, one is lost in admiration at the facilities for inter-communication which are thus provided for the future inhabitants of this wonderful region. It is true at the present moment they lie unused except by the Indian fisherman and villager, but the day will surely come when the rapidly diminishing stores of pine upon this continent will be still further exhausted, and when the nations of Europe as well as of America will be obliged to recur to British Columbia for a material of which you will, by that time, be the principal depository. Already from an adjoining port on the mainland a large trade is being done in lumber with Great Britain, Europe, Australia, and South America, and I venture to think that ere long the ports of the United States will perforce be thrown open to your traffic.

I had the pleasure of witnessing the overthrow by the axes of your woodmen of one of your forest giants, that towered to the height of two hundred and fifty feet above our heads, and whose rings bore witness that it dated its origin from the reign of the fourth Edward, and where it grew, and for thousands of miles along the coast beyond it, millions of its contemporaries are awaiting the same fate. With such facilities of access as I have described to the heart and centre of your various forest lands, where almost every tree can be rolled from the spot upon which it grew to the ship which is to transfer it to its destination, it would be difficult to over-estimate the opportunities of industrial development thus indicated; and to prove that I am not over-sanguine in my conjectures, I will read you a letter recently received from the British Admiralty by Mr. Innes, the Superintendent of the Dockyard at Esquimalt:—

"From various causes spars from

Canada, the former main source of supply, have not of late years been obtainable, and the trade in New Zealand spars for topmasts has also completely died away. Of late years the sole source of supply has been the casual cargoes of Oregon spars, imported from time to time, and from these the wants of the Services have been met. But my Lords feel that this is not a mode to be depended upon, more especially for the larger sized spars."

Their Lordships then proceed to order Mr. Innes to make arrangements for the transhipment for the dockyards of Great Britain of the specifical number of Douglas pine which will be required by the service during the ensuing year—and what England does in this direction other nations will feel themselves bound to do as well. But I have learnt a further lesson; I have had opportunities of inspecting some of the spots where your mineral wealth is stored, and here again the ocean stands your friend, the mouths of the coal-pits I have visited almost opening into the hulls of the vessels which are to convey their contents across the ocean. When it is further remembered that inexhaustible supplies of iron ore are found in juxtaposition with your coal, no one can blame you for regarding the beautiful island on which you live as having been especially favoured by Providence in the distribution of these natural gifts.

But still more precious minerals than either coal or iron ore enhance the value your possessions. As we skirted the banks of the Fraser, we were met at every turn by evidences of its extraordinary supplies of fish; but scarcely less frequent were the signs afforded us of the golden treasures it rolls down, nor need any traveller think it strange to see the Indian fisherman hauling out a salmon on to the sands from whence a miner beside him is sifting the sparkling ore. But the signs of mineral wealth which may happen to have attracted my personal attention are as nothing, I understand, to what is exhibited in Cariboo, Casslar, and along the valley of the Stickeen ; and most grieved am I to think that I have not had time to testify, by my presence amongst them, to the sympathy I feel with the adventurous prospector and the miner in their arduous enterprises. I had also the satisfaction of having pointed out to me where various lodes of silver only await greater facilities of access to be worked with profit and advantage. But, perhaps, the greatest surprise in store for us was the discovery, on our exit from the Pass through the Cascade Range, of the noble expanse of pastoral lands, and the long vistas of fertile valleys which opened up on every side as we advanced through the country, and which, as I could see with my own eyes from various heights we traversed, extend in rounded upland slopes, or in gentle depressions for hundreds of miles to the foot of the Rocky Mountains, proving, after all, that the mountain ranges which frown along your coast no more accurately indicate the nature of the territory they guard than does the wall of breaking surf that roars along a tropic beach presage the softly undulating sea that glitters in the sun beyond.

But you will very likely say to me, of what service to us are these resources which you describe, if they, and we, are to remain locked up in a distant, and, at present inaccessible corner of the Dominion, cut off by a trackless waste of intervening territory from all intercourse, whether of a social or of a commercial character, with those with whom we are politically united? Well, gentlemen, I can only answer: Of comparatively little use, or, at all events, of far less profit than they would immediately become, were the railway, upon whose construction you naturally counted when you entered into Confederation, once completed. But here I feel I am touching upon dangerous ground. You are well aware that from the first moment I set foot in the Province, I was careful to inform everyone who approached me that I came here as Governor-General of the Dominion, the representative of Her Majesty, exactly in the same way as I had passed through other Provinces of the Dominion, in order to make acquaintance with the people, their wants, wishes, and aspirations, and to learn as much as I could in regard to the physical features, capabilities, and resources of the Province, that I had not come on a diplomatic mission, or as a messenger, or charged with any announcement, either from the Imperial or from the Dominion Government. This statement I beg now most distinctly to repeat. Nor should it be imagined that I have come either to persuade or coax you into any line of action which you may not consider conducive to your own interests, or to make any new promises on behalf of my Government, or renew any old ones; least of all have I a design to force upon you any further modification of those arrangements which were arrived at in 1874 between the Provincial and the Dominion Governments under the auspices of Lord Carnarvon. Should any business of this kind have to be perfected, it will be done in the usual constitutional manner through the Secretary of State. But, though I have thought it well thus unmistakably and effectually to guard against my journey to the Province being misinterpreted, there is, I admit, one mission with which I am charged—a mission that it is strictly within my functions to fulfil— namely, the mission of testifying by my presence amongst you and by my patient and respectful attention to everything which may be said to me, that the Government and the entire people of Canada, without distinction of party, are most sincerely desirous of cultivating with you those friendly and affectionate relations, upon the existence of which must depend the future harmony and solidity of our common Dominion.

Gentlemen, this mission I think you will admit I have done my best to fulfil. I think you will bear me witness that I have been inaccessible to no one—that I have shown neither impatience nor indifference during the conversations I have had with you—and that it would have been impossible for anyone to have exhibited more anxiety thoroughly to understand your views. I think it will be further admitted that I have done this, without in the slightest degree seeking to disturb or embarrass the march of your domestic politics. I have treated the existing Ministers as it became me to treat the responsible advisers of the Crown in this locality, and I have shown that deference to their opponents which is always due to Her Majesty's Loyal Opposition. Nay, further, I think it must have been observed that I have betrayed no disposition either to create or foment in what might be termed, though most incorrectly, the interest of Canada, any discord or contrariety of interest between the mainland and the island. Such a mode of procedure would have been most unworthy; for no true friend of the Dominion should be capable of any other object or desire than to give universal satisfaction to the Province as a whole.

A settlement of the pending controversy would indeed be most lamely concluded if it left either of the sections into which your community is geographically divided, unsatisfied. Let me then assure you on the part of the Canadian Government, and on the part of the Canadian people at large, that there is nothing they desire more earnestly or more fervently than to know and feel that you are one with them in heart, thought, and feeling. Canada would indeed be dead to the most self-evident considerations of self-interest and to the first instincts of national pride, if she did not regard with satisfaction her connection with a Province so richly endowed by nature, inhabited by a community so replete with British loyalty and pluck, while it afforded her the means of extending her confines and the outlets of her commerce to the wide Pacific and the countries beyond. It is true, circumstances have arisen to create an unfriendly and hostile feeling in your minds against Canada. You consider yourselves injured, and you certainly have been disappointed. Far be it from me to belittle your grievances, or to speak slightingly of your complaints.

Happily my independent position relieves me from the necessity of engaging with you in any irritating discussion upon the various points which are in controversy between this colony and the Dominion Government. On the contrary, I am ready to make several admissions. I don't suppose that in any part of Canada will it be denied that you have been subjected both to anxiety and uncertainty on points which were of vital importance to you. From first to last since the idea of a Pacific railway was originated, things, to use a homely phrase, have gone "contrairy" with it, and with everybody connected with it, and you, in common, with many other persons, have suffered in many ways. But though happily it is no part of my duty to pronounce judgment in these matters, or to approve, or blame, or criticise the conduct of any one concerned, I think that I can render both Canada and British Columbia some service by speaking to certain matters of fact which have taken place within my own immediate cognizance, and by thus removing from your minds certain wrong impressions in regard to those matters of fact which have undoubtedly taken deep root there. Now, gentlemen, in discharging this task, I may also call it this duty, I am sure my observations will be received by those I see around me in a candid and loyal spirit, and that the heats and passions which have been engendered by these unhappy differences will not prove an impediment to a calm consideration of what I am about to say, more especially as it will be my endeavour to avoid wounding any susceptibilities, or forcing upon your attention views or opinions which may be ungrateful to you. Of course, I well understand that the gravamen of the charge against the Canadian Government is that it has failed to fulfil its treaty engagements. Those engagements were embodied in a solemn agreement which was ratified by the respective Legislatures of the contracting parties, who were at the time perfectly independent of each other, and I admit they thus acquired all the characteristics of an international treaty.

The terms of that treaty were (to omit the minor items) that Canada undertook to secure within two years from the date of union the simultaneous commencement at either end of a railway which was to connect the seaboard of British Columbia with the railway system of the Dominion, and that such railway should be completed within ten years from the date of union in 1871. We are now in 1876. Five years have elapsed, and the work of construction, even at one end, can be said to have only just begun. Undoubtedly under these circumstances everyone must allow that Canada has failed to fulfil her treaty obligations towards this Province, but unfortunately Canada has been accused not only of failing to accomplish her undertakings, but of what is a very different thing—a wilful breach of faith in having neglected to do so. Well, let us consider for a moment whether this very serious assertion is true. What was the state of things when the bargain was made? At that time everything in Canada was prosperous; her finances were flourishing, the discovery of the great North-west, so to speak, had inflamed her imagination. Above all things, railway enterprise in the United States and generally on this continent was being developed to an astounding extent. One trans-continental railway had been successfully executed, and several others on the same gigantic scale were being projected. It had come to be considered that a railway could be flung across the Rocky Mountains as readily as across a hay-field, and the observations of those who passed from New York and San Francisco did not suggest any extraordinary obstacles to undertakings of the description.

Unfortunately one element in the calculation was left entirely out of account, and that was the comparative ignorance which prevailed in regard to the character of our Northern Ranges, and the mountain passes which intervened between the Hudson's Bay Company's possessions and the Western coast. In the United States, for years and years, troops of emigrants had passed westward to Salt Lake City, to Sacramento, and to the Golden Gate; every track and trail through the mountains was wayworn and well-known; the location of a line in that neighbourhood was pre-determined by the experience of persons already well acquainted with the locality. But in our case the trans-continental passes were sparse and unfrequented, and from an engineering point of view may be said to have been absolutely unknown. It was under these circumstances that Canada undertook to commence her Pacific Railway in two years, and to finish it in ten. In doing this she undoubtedly pledged herself to that which was a physical impossibility, for the moment the engineers peered over the Rocky Mountains into your Province, they saw at once that before any one passage through the devious range before them could be pronounced the best, an amount of preliminary surveying would have to be undertaken which it would require several years to complete. Now there is a legal motto which says *nemo tenetur ad impossibile*, and I would submit to you that under the circumstances I have mentioned, however great the default of Canada, she need not necessarily have been guilty of any wilful breach of faith. I myself am quite convinced that when Canada ratified this bargain with you she acted in perfect good faith, and fully believed that she would accomplish her promise, if not within ten years, at all events within such a sufficiently reasonable period as would satisfy your requirements. The mistake she made was in being too sanguine in her calculations; but remember, a portion of the blame for concluding a bargain, impossible of accomplishment, cannot be confined to one only of the parties to it. The mountains which have proved our stumbling block were your own mountains, and within your own territory, and however deeply an impartial observer might sympathize with you in the miscarriage of the two time terms of the compact, one of which—namely as to the commencement of the line in two years from 1871—has failed, and the other of which, namely, its completion in ten, must fail, it is impossible to forget that yourselves are by no means without responsibility for such a result.

It is quite true—in what I must admit to be a most generous spirit—you intimated in various ways that you did not desire to hold Canada too strictly to the letter of her engagements as to time. Your expectations in this respect were stated by your late Lieutenant-Governor, Mr. Trutch, very fairly and explicitly, though a very unfair use has been made of his words, and I have no doubt that if unforeseen circumstances had not intervened, you would have exhibited as much patience as could have been expected of you. But a serious crisis supervened in the political career of Canada—Sir John Macdonald resigned office, and Mr. Mackenzie acceded to power, and to all the responsibilities incurred by Canada in respect to you and your Province. Now it is asserted, and I imagine with truth, that Mr. Mackenzie and his political friends had always been opposed to many portions of Canada's bargain with British Columbia. It therefore came to be considered in this Province that the new Government was an enemy to the Pacific Railway; but I believe this to have been and to be a complete misapprehension. I believe the Pacific Railway has no better friend in Canada than Mr. Mackenzie, and that he was only opposed to the time terms in the bargain, because he believed them impossible of accomplishment, and that a conscientious endeavour to ·fulfil them would unnecessarily and ruinously increase the finanical expenditure of the country, and in both these opinions Mr. Mackenzie was undoubtedly right.

With the experience we now possess, and of course it is easy to be wise after the event, no one would dream of saying that the Railway could have been surveyed, located, and built within the period named, or that any company who might undertake to build the line within that period would not have required double or treble the bonus that would have been sufficient had construction been arranged for at a more leisurely rate ; but surely it would be both ungenerous and unreasonable for British Columbia to entertain any hostile feelings towards Mr. Mackenzie on this account, nor is he to be blamed, in my opinion, if, on entering office in so unexpected a manner, he took time to consider the course which he would pursue in regard to his mode of dealing with a question of such enormous importance. His position was undoubtedly a very embarrassing one, his Government had inherited responsibilities which he knew, and which the country had come to know, could not be discharged. Already British Columbia had begun to cry out for the fulfilment of the bargain, and that at the very time that Canada had reached the conclusion that a relaxation of some of its conditions was necessary. Out of such a condition of affairs it was almost impossible but that there should arise in the first place delay—for all changes of Government necessarily check the progress of public business—and in the next friction, controversy, collision, between the Province and the Dominion.

Happily it is not necessary that I should follow the current of that quarrel or discuss the curious points which were then contested. You cannot expect me to make any admissions in respect to the course my Ministers may have thought it right to pursue, nor would it be gracious upon my part to criticise the action of your Province during this painful period. Out of the altercation which then ensued there issued under the auspices of Lord Carnarvon—a settlement; and when an agreement has been arrived at the sooner the incidents connected with the conflict which preceded it are forgotten, the better Here then we have arrived at a new era; the former laches of Canada, if any such there had been, are abandoned, and the two time terms of the treaty are relaxed on the one part, while on the other specific obligations are superadded to the main Article in the original bargain: that is to say—again omitting minor items—the Province agreed to the Pacific Railway being completed in sixteen years from 1874, and to its being begun "as soon as the surveys shall have been completed," instead of at a fixed date, while the Dominion Government undertook to construct at once a railway from Esquimalt to Nanaimo, to hurry forward the surveys with the utmost possible dispatch, and as soon as construction should have begun, to spend two millions a year in the prosecution of the work.

I find that in this part of the world these arrangements have come to be known as the "Carnarvon Terms." It is a very convenient designation, and I am quite content to adopt it on one condition, namely, that Lord Carnarvon is not to be saddled with any of the original responsibility with regard to any of these terms but one. The main body of the terms are Mr. Mackenzie's; that is to say, Mr. Mackenzie proffered the Nanaimo and Esquimalt railway, the telegraph line, the waggon-road, and the annual expenditure. All that Lord Carnarvon did was to suggest that the proposed expenditure should be two millions instead of one million and a half, and that a time-limit should be added. But, as you are well aware, this last condition was necessarily implied in the preceding one relating to the annual expenditure—for once committed to that expenditure, Canada would in self-defence be obliged to hasten the completion of the line in order to render reproductive the capital she sank as quickly as possible. It is, therefore, but just to Lord Carnarvon that he should be absolved from the responsibility of having been in any way the inventor of what are known as the "Carnarvon Terms." Lord Carnarvon merely did what every arbitrator would do under the circumstances; he found the parties already agreed in respect to the principal items of the bargain, and was consequently relieved from pronouncing on their intrinsic merits, and proceeded at once to suggest to Canada the further concession which would be necessary to bring her into final accord with her opponent. In pursuance of this agreement the Canadian Government organized a series of surveying parties upon a most extensive and costly scale. In fact, during the last two years two millions of money alone have been expended on these operations. The Chief Engineer himself has told me that Mr. Mackenzie had given him *carte blanche* in the matter, so anxious was he to have the route determined without delay, and that the mountains were already as full of as many theodolites and surveyors as they could hold.

I am aware it is asserted, indeed as much has been said to me since I came here, that these surveys were merely multiplied in order to furnish an excuse for further delays. Well, that is rather a hard saying. But upon this point I can speak from my own personal knowledge, and I am sure that what I say on this head will be accepted as the absolute truth. During the whole of the period under review, I was in constant personal communication with Mr. Fleming, was kept acquainted by that gentleman with everything that was being done. I knew the position of every surveying party in the area under examination. Now Mr. Fleming is a gentleman in whose personal integrity and in whose professional ability everyone I address has the most perfect confidence. Mr. Fleming, of course, was the responsible engineer who planned those surveys and determined the lines along which they were to be carried, and over and over again Mr. Fleming has explained to me how unexpected were the difficulties he had to encounter; how repeatedly after following hopefully a particular route his engineers found themselves stopped by an impassable wall of mountain which blocked the way, and how trail after trail had to be examined and abandoned before he had hit on anything like a practicable route. Even now, after all that has been done, a glance at the map will show you how devious and erratic is the line which appears to afford the only tolerable exit from the labyrinthine ranges of the Cascades.

Notwithstanding, therefore, whatever may have been bruited abroad in the sense to which I have alluded, I am sure it will be admitted, nay, I know it is admitted, that so far as the prosecution of the surveys is concerned, Canada has used due diligence, yes, more than due diligence in her desire to comply with that section of the "Carnarvon Terms" relating to this particular. You must remember that it is a matter of the greatest moment, affecting the success of the entire scheme, and calculated permanently to affect the future destiny of the people of Canada, that a right decision should be arrived at in regard to the location of the western portion of the line, and a Minister would be a traitor to a most sacred trust if he allowed himself to be teased, intimidated, or cajoled into any precipitate decision on such a momentous point until every possible route had been duly examined. When I left Ottawa, the engineers seemed disposed to report that our ultimate choice would lie between two routes, both starting from Fort George, namely, that which leads to the head of Dean's Canal, and that which terminates in Bute Inlet. Of these two the line to Dean's Canal was the shortest by some forty miles, and was considerably the cheaper by reason of its easier grades. The ultimate exit of this channel to the sea was also more direct than the tortuous navigation out of Bute Inlet; but Mr. Mackenzie added—though you must not take what I am now going to say as a definite conclusion on his part, or an authoritative communication upon mine—that provided the difference in expense was not so great as to forbid it, he would desire to adopt what might be the less advantageous route from the Dominion point of view, in order to follow that line which would most aptly meet the requirements of the Province.

Without pronouncing an opinion on the merits of either of the routes, which it is no part of my business to do, I may venture to say that in this principle I think Mr. Mackenzie is right, and that it would be wise and generous of Canada to consult the local interests of British Columbia by bringing the line and its terminus within reach of existing settlements, if it can be done without any undue sacrifice of public money. From a recent article in the " Globe," it would seem as though Bute Inlet line had finally found favour with the Government, though I myself have no information on the point, and I am happy to see from the statistics furnished by that journal, that not only has the entire line to the Pacific been at last surveyed, located, graded, and its profile taken out, but that the calculated expenses of construction, though very great, and to be incurred only after careful consideration, are far less than were anticipated. Well, gentlemen, should the indications we have received of the intentions of the Government prove correct, you are very much to be congratulated, for I am well aware that the line to Bute Inlet is the one you have always favoured, and I should hope that now at last you will be satisfied that the Canadian Government has strained every nerve, as it undertook to do, to fulfil to the letter its first and principal obligation under the Carnarvon Terms, by prosecuting with the utmost despatch the surveys of the line to the Pacific Coast. I only wish that Waddington Harbour, at the head of the Inlet, was a better port. I confess to having but a very poor opinion of it, and certainly the acquaintance I have made with Seymour Narrows and the intervening channels which will have to be bridged or ferried, did not seem to me to be very favourable to either operation.

Well, then, we now come to the Esquimalt and Nanaimo Railway. I am well aware of the extraordinary importance you attach to this work, and of course I am perfectly ready to admit that its immediate execution was promised to you in the most definite and absolute manner under Lord Carnarvon's arbitration. I am not, therefore, surprised at the irritation and excitement occasioned in this city by the non-fulfilment of this item in the agreement—nay, I will go further, I think it extremely natural that the miscarriage of this part of the bargain should have been provocative of very strenuous language and deeply embittered feelings, nor am I surprised that as is almost certain to follow on such occasions, you should in your vexation put a very injurious construction on the conduct of those who had undertaken to realize your hopes; but still I know that I am addressing high-minded and reasonable men, and, moreover, that you are perfectly convinced that I would sooner cut my right hand off than utter a single word that I do not know to be an absolute truth.

Two years have passed since the Canadian Government undertook to commence the construction of the Esquimalt and Nanaimo Railway, and the Nanaimo and Esquimalt Railway is not even commenced, and what is more, there does not at present seem a prospect of its being commenced. What, then, is the history of your case, and who is answerable for your disappointment? I know you consider Mr. Mackenzie. I am not here to defend Mr. Mackenzie, his policy, his proceedings, or his utterances. I hope this will be clearly understood. In anything I have hitherto said I have done nothing of this sort, nor do I intend to do so. I have merely stated to you certain matters with which I thought it well for you to be acquainted, because they have been misapprehended, and what I now tell you are also matters of fact within my own cognizance, and which have no relation to Mr. Mackenzie as the head of a political party, and I tell them to you not only in your own interest, but in the interest of public morality and English honour. In accordance with his engagements to you in relation to the Nanaimo and Esquimalt Railway, Mr. Mackenzie introduced as soon as it was possible a Bill into the Canadian House of Commons, the clauses of which were admitted by your representatives in Parliament fully to discharge his obligations to yourselves and to Lord Carnarvon in respect to that undertaking, and carried it through the Lower House by a large majority. I have reason to think that many of his supporters voted for the Bill with very great misgivings both as to the policy of the measure and the intrinsic merits of the railway, but their leader had pledged himself to exercise his Parliamentary influence to pass it, and they very properly carried it through for him. It went up to the Senate, and was thrown out by that body by a majority of two. Well, I have learnt with regret that there is a very widespread conviction in this community that Mr. Mackenzie had surreptitiously procured the defeat of his own measure in the Upper House. Had Mr. Mackenzie dealt so treacherously by Lord Carnarvon, by the Representative of his Sovereign in this country, or by you, he would have been guilty of a most atrocious act, of which I trust no public man in Canada or in any other British Colony could be capable. I tell you in the most emphatic terms, and I pledge my own honour on the point, that Mr. Mackenzie was not guilty of any such base and deceitful conduct—had I thought him guilty of it, either he would have ceased to be Prime Minister or I should have left the country.

But the very contrary was the fact. While these events were passing I was in constant personal communication with Mr. Mackenzie, I naturally watched the progress of the Bill with the greatest anxiety, because I was aware of the eagerness with which the Act was desired in Victoria, and because I had long felt the deepest sympathy with you in the succession of disappointments to which, by the force of circumstances, you had been exposed. When the Bill passed the House of Commons by a large majority with the assent of the leader of the Opposition, in common with everyone else, I concluded it was safe, and the adverse vote of the Senate took me as much by surprise as it did you and the rest of the world. I saw Mr. Mackenzie the next day, and I have seldom seen a man more annoyed or disconcerted than he was; indeed he was driven at that interview to protest with more warmth than he had ever used against the decision of the English Government, which had refused, on the opinion of the law officers of the Crown, to allow him to add to the members of the Senate, when, soon after his accession to office, Prince Edward Island had entered Confederation.

"Had I been permitted," he said to me, " to exercise my rights in that respect this would not have happened, but how can these mischances be prevented in a body the majority of which, having been nominated by my political opponent, is naturally hostile to me?"

Now, gentlemen, your acquaintance

with Parliamentary Government must tell you that this last observation of Mr. Mackenzie's was a perfectly just one. But my attention has been drawn to the fact that two of Mr. Mackenzie's party supported his Conservative opponents in the rejection of the Bill, but surely you don't imagine that a Prime Minister can deal with his supporters in the Senate as if they were a regiment of soldiers. In the House of Commons he has a better chance of maintaining party discipline, for the constituencies are very apt to resent any insubordination on the part of their members towards the leader of their choice. But a Senator is equally independent of the Crown, the Minister, or the people; and as in the House of Lords at home, so in the Second Chamber in Canada, gentlemen will run from time to time on the wrong side of the post.

But it has been observed—granting that the two members in question did not vote as they did at Mr. Mackenzie's instigation—he has exhibited his perfidy in not sending in his resignation as soon as the Senate had pronounced against the Bill. Now, gentlemen, you cannot expect me to discuss Mr. Mackenzie's conduct in that respect. It would be very improper for me to do' so; but though I cannot discuss Mr. Mackenzie's conduct, I am perfectly at liberty to tell you what I myself should have done had Mr. Mackenzie tendered to me his resignation. I should have told him that in my opinion such a course was quite unjustifiable, that as the House of Commons was then constituted I saw no prospect of the Queen's Government being advantageously carried on except under his leadership, and that were he to resign at that time, the greatest inconvenience and detriment would ensue to the public service. That is what I should have said to Mr. Mackenzie in the event contemplated, and I have no doubt that the Parliament and the people of Canada would have confirmed my decision.

But it has been furthermore urged that

Mr. Mackenzie ought to have re-introduced the Bill. Well, that is again a point I cannot discuss, but I may tell you this, that if Mr. Mackenzie had done so, I very much doubt whether he would have succeeded in carrying it a second time even in the House of Commons. The fact is that Canada at large, whether rightly or wrongly I do not say, has unmistakably shown its approval of the vote in the Senate. An opinion has come to prevail from one end of the Dominion to the other, an opinion which I find is acquiesced in by a considerable proportion of the inhabitants of British Columbia, that the Nanaimo and Esquimalt Railway cannot stand upon its own merits, and that its construction as a Government enterprise would be at all events at present a useless expenditure of the public money. Now again let me assure you that I am not presuming to convey to you any opinion of my own on this much contested point. Even did I entertain any misgivings on the subject it would be very ungracious for me to parade them in your presence and on such an occasion. I am merely communicating to you my conjecture why it is that Mr. Mackenzie has shown no signs of his intention to re-introduce the Nanaimo and Esquimalt Railway Bill into Parliament, viz.—because he had no chance of getting it passed.

Well, then, gentlemen, of whom and what have you to complain? Well, you have every right from your point of view to complain of the Canadian Senate. You have a right to say that after the Government of the day had promised that a measure upon which a majority of the inhabitants of an important Province had set their hearts should be passed, it was ill-advised and unhandsome of that body not to confirm the natural expectations which had thus been engendered in your breasts, especially when that work was itself offered as a *solatium* to you for a previous injury. I fully admit that it is a very grave step for either House of the Legislature, and particularly for that which is not the popular branch, to disavow any agreement into which the Executive may have entered, except under a very absolute sense of public duty. Mind, I am not saying that this is not such a case, but I say that you have got a perfect right, from your own point of view, not so to regard it. But, gentlemen, that is all. You have got no right to go beyond that. You have got no right to describe yourselves as a second time the victims of a broken agreement.

As I have shown you, the persons who had entered into an engagement in regard to this railway with you and Lord Carnarvon had done their very best to discharge their obligation. But the Senate, who counteracted their intention, had given no preliminary promises whatsoever, either to you or to the Secretary of State. They rejected the Bill in the legitimate exercise of their constitutional functions, and there is nothing more to be said on this head so far as that body is concerned, either by you or Lord Carnarvon, for I need not assure you that there is not the slightest chance that any Secretary of State in Downing Street would attempt anything so unconstitutional—so likely to kindle a flame throughout the whole Dominion—as to coerce the free legislative action of her Legislature. But there is one thing I admit the Senate has done. It has revived in their integrity those original treaty obligations on the strength of which you were induced to enter confederation, and it has re-imposed upon Mr. Mackenzie and his Government the obligation of offering you an equivalent for that stipulation in the " Carnarvon Terms" which he has not been able to make good.

Now, from the very strong language which has been used in regard to the conduct of Mr. Mackenzie, a bystander would be led to imagine that as soon as his Railway Bill had miscarried, he had cynically refused to take any further action in the matter. Had my Government done this they would have exposed themselves to the severest reprehension, and such conduct would have been both faithless to you and disrespectful to Lord Carnarvon; but so far from having acted in this manner, Mr. Mackenzie has offered you a very considerable grant of money in consideration of your disappointment. Now here again I won't touch upon the irritating controversies which have circled round this particular step in these transactions. I am well aware that you consider this offer to have been made under conditions of which you have reason to complain. If this has been the case it is most unfortunate, but still, whatever may have been the sinister incidents connected with the past, the one solid fact remains that the Canadian Government has offered you seven hundred and fifty thousand dollars in lieu of the railway. This sum has been represented to me as totally inadequate, and as very short of an equivalent. It may be so, or it may not be so. Neither upon that point will I offer an opinion, but still I may mention to you the principle upon which that sum has been arrived at.

Under the Nanaimo and Esquimalt Railway Bill, whose rejection by the Senate we have been considering, Canada was to contribute a bonus of ten thousand dollars a mile; the total distance of the line is about seventy miles, consequently the seven hundred and fifty thousand dollars is nothing more nor less than this very bonus converted into a lump sum. Now, since I have come here, it has been represented to me by the friends of the railway that it is a line which is capable of standing on its own merits, and that a company had been almost induced to take it up some time ago as an unsubsidized enterprise. Nay, only yesterday, the local paper, which is the most strenuous champion for the line, asserted that it could be built for two million dollars; that the lands—which, with the seven hundred and fifty thousand dollars, were to be replaced by Mr. Mackenzie at your disposal — were worth several millions more, and that the railway itself would prove a most paying concern. If this is so—and what better authority can I refer to?—is it not obvious that the bonus proposal of the Dominion Government assumes at least the semblance of a fair offer, and even if you did not consider it absolutely up to the mark, it should not have been denounced in the very strong language which has been used.

However, I do not wish to discuss the point whether the seven hundred and fifty thousand dollars was a sufficient offer or not. I certainly am not empowered to hold out to you any hopes of an advance; all that I would venture to sumbit is that Mr. Mackenzie, having been thwarted in his *bonâ fide* endeavour to fulfil this special item in the "Carnarvon Terms," has adopted the only course left to him in proposing to discharge his obligations by a money payment. I confess I should have thought this would be the most natural solution of the problem, and that the payment of a sum of money equivalent to the measure of Mr. Mackenzie's original obligation, to be expended under whatever conditions would be most immediately advantageous to the Province and ultimately beneficial to the Dominion, would not have been an unnatural remedy for the misadventure which has stultified this special stipulation in regard to the Nanaimo and Esquimalt Railway; but, of course, of these matters you yourselves are the best judges, and I certainly have not the slightest desire to suggest to you any course which you may think contrary to your interests. My only object in touching upon them at all is to disabuse your minds of the idea that there has been any intention upon the part of Mr. Mackenzie, his Government, or of Canada to break their faith with you. Every single item of the "Carnarvon Terms" is at this moment in the course of fulfilment. At enormous expense the surveys have been pressed forward to completion, the fifty millions of land and the thirty millions of money to be provided for by Canada under the Bill are ready, the profiles of the main line have been taken out, and the most elaborate information has been sent over to Europe in regard to every section of the country through which it passes; several thousand miles of the stipulated telegraph have been laid down, and now that the location of the western terminus seems to have been determined, though upon this point I have myself no information, tenders, I imagine, will be called for almost immediately. Whatever further steps may be necessary to float the undertaking as a commercial enterprise will be adopted, and the promised waggon-road will necessarily follow *pari passu* with construction.

Well, then, gentlemen, how will you stand under these circumstances? You will have got your line to Bute Inlet. Now I will communicate to you a conclusion I have arrived at from my visit to that locality. If the Pacific Railway once comes to Bute Inlet it cannot stop there. It may pause there for a considerable time, until Canadian trans-Pacific traffic with Australia, China, and Japan shall have begun to expand, but such a traffic once set going, Waddington Harbour will no longer serve as a terminal port; in fact it is no harbour at all and scarcely an anchorage—the railway must be prolonged under these circumstances to Esquimalt, that is to say if the deliberate opinion of the engineers should pronounce the operation feasible, and Canada shall in the meantime have acquired the additional financial stability which would justify her undertaking what, under any circumstances, must prove one of the most gigantic achievements the world has ever witnessed. In that case, of course, the Nanaimo Railway springs into existence of its own accord, and you will then be in possession both of your money compensation and of the thing for which it was paid, and with this result I do not think you should be ill-satisfied. But should the contrary be the case, the prospect is indeed a gloomy one; should hasty counsels and the exhibition of an impracticable spirit throw these arrangements into confusion, interrupt or change our present railway programme, and necessitate any re-arrangement of your political relations, I fear Victoria would be the chief sufferer. I scarcely like to allude to such a contingency, nor, gentlemen, are my observations directed immediately to you, for I know very well that neither those whom I am addressing, nor do the great majority of the inhabitants of Vancouver Island or of Victoria, participate in the views to which I am about to refer, but still a certain number of your fellow-citizens, gentlemen, with whom I have had a great deal of pleasant and interesting conversation, and who have shown to me personally the greatest kindness and courtesy, have sought to impress me with the belief that if the Legislature of Canada is not compelled by some means or other, which, however, they do not specify, to make forthwith these seventy miles of railway, they will be strong enough, in the face of Mr. Mackenzie's offer of a money equivalent, to take British Columbia out of the Confederation. Well, they certainly won't be able to do that. I am now in a position to judge for myself as to what are the real sentiments of the community. I will even presume to say I know more about it than these gentlemen themselves. When once the main line of the Pacific Railway is under way, the whole population of the Mainland would be perfectly contented with the present situation of affairs, and will never dream of detaching their fortunes from those of Her Majesty's great Dominion. Nay, I don't believe that these gentlemen would be able to persuade their fellow citizens even of the Island of Vancouver to so violent a course; but granting for the moment that their influence should prevail—what would be the result? British Columbia would still be part and parcel of Canada. The great work of Confederation would not be perceptibly affected, but the proposed line of the Pacific Railway might possibly be deflected south. New Westminster would certainly become the capital of the Province, the Dominion would naturally use its best endeavours to build it up into a flourishing and prosperous city. It would be the seat of Government, and the home of justice, as well as the chief social centre on the Pacific coast. Burrard Inlet would become a great commercial port, and the miners of Cariboo, with their stores of gold dust, would spend their festive and open-handed winters there. Great Britain would, of course, retain Esquimalt as a naval station on this coast, as she has retained Halifax as a naval station on the other, and inasmuch as a constituency of some one thousand five hundred persons would not be able to supply the material for a Parliamentary Government, Vancouver and its inhabitants, who are now influential by reason of their intelligence rather than their numbers, would be ruled as Jamaica, Malta, Gibraltar, Heligoland, and Ascension are ruled, through the instrumentality of some naval or other officer. Nanaimo would become the principal town of the Island, and Victoria would lapse for many a long year into the condition of a village, until the development of your coalfields and the growth of a healthier sentiment had prepared the way for its re-incorporation with the rest of the Province; at least, that is the horoscope I should draw for it in the contingency contemplated by these gentlemen.

But God forbid that any such prophecy should be realized. I believe the gentlemen I have referred to are the very last who would desire to see the fulfilment of their menaces, and I hope they will forgive me if I am not intimidated by their formidable representations. When some pertinacious philosopher insisted on assailing the late King of the Belgians with a rhapsody on the beauties of a Republican Government, His Majesty replied, "You forget, Sir, that I am a Royalist by profession." Well, a Governor-General is a Federalist by profession, and you might as well expect the Sultan of Turkey to throw up his cap for the Commune as the Viceroy of Canada to entertain a suggestion for the disintegration of the Dominion.

I hope, therefore, they will not bear me any ill will for having declined to bow my head beneath their "separation" arch. It was a very good-humoured, and certainly not a disloyal bit of "bounce" which they had prepared for me. I suppose they wished me to know they were the "arch" enemies of Canada. Well, I have made them an arch reply. But, gentlemen, of course I am not serious in discussing such a contingency as that to which I have referred. Your numerical weakness as a community is your real strength, for it is a consideration which appeals to every generous heart. Far be the day when on any acre of soil above which floats the flag of England, mere material power, brute political preponderance should be permitted to decide such a controversy as that which we are discussing. It is to men like yourselves who, with unquailing fortitude and heroic energy have planted the laws and liberties and the blessed influences of English homes amidst the wilds and desert plains of savage lands, that England owes the enhancement of her prestige, the diffusion of her tongue, the increase of her commerce and her ever-widening renown, and woe betide the Government or Statesman who, because its inhabitants are few in number and politically of small account, should disregard the wishes or carelessly dismiss the representations however bluff, boisterous or downright, of the feeblest of our distant colonies. No, gentlemen, neither England nor Canada would be content or happy in any settlement that was not arrived at with your own hearty approval and consent, and equally satisfactory to every section of your Province; but we appeal to your moderation and practical good sense to assist us in resolving the present difficulty. The genius of the English race has ever been too robust and sensible to admit the existence of an irreconcilable element in its midst. It is only among weak and hysterical populations that such a growth can flourish. However hard the blows given and taken during the contest, Britishers always find a means of making up the quarrel, and such I trust will be the case on the present occasion. My functions, as a constitutional ruler, are simply to superintend the working of the political machine, but not to intermeddle with its action. I trust that I have observed that rule on the present occasion, and that, although I have addressed you at considerable length, I have not said a word which it has not been strictly within my province to say, or intruded on those domains which are reserved for my responsible advisers. As I warned you would be the case, I have made no announcement, I have made no promise, I have hazarded no opinion upon any of the administrative questions now occupying the joint attention of yourselves and the Dominion. I have only endeavoured to correct some misapprehensions by which you have been possessed in regard to matters of historical fact, and I have testified to the kind feeling entertained for you by your fellow-subjects in Canada, and to the desire of my Government for the re-establishment of the friendliest and kindest relations between you and themselves; and I trust that I may carry away with me the conviction that from henceforth a less angry and irritated feeling towards Canada will have been inaugurated than has hitherto subsisted. Of my own earnest desire to do anything I can to forward your views, so far as they may be founded in justice and reason, I need not speak. My presence here and the way in which I have spent my time will have convinced you of what has been the object nearest my heart. I cannot say how glad I am to have come or how much I have profited by my visit, and I assure you none of the representations with which I have been favoured will escape my memory or fail to be duly submitted in the proper quarter.

And now, gentlemen, I must bid you

good-bye; but before doing so there is one other topic upon which I am desirous of touching. From my first arrival in Canada, I have been very much preoccupied with the condition of the Indian population in this Province. You must remember that the Indian populations are not represented in Parliament, and consequently that the Governor-General is bound to watch over their welfare with special solicitude. Now, we must all admit that the condition of the Indian question in British Columbia is not satisfactory. Most unfortunately, as I think, there has been an initial error ever since Sir James Douglas quitted office, in the Government of British Columbia neglecting to recognize what is known as the Indian title. In Canada this has always been done; no Government, whether provincial or central, has failed to acknowledge that the original title to the land existed in the Indian tribes and communities that hunted or wandered over it. Before we touch an acre we make a treaty with the chiefs representing the bands we are dealing with, and having agreed upon and paid the stipulated price, oftentimes arrived at after a great deal of haggling and difficulty, we enter into possession, but not until then do we consider that we are entitled to deal with an acre. The result has been that in Canada our Indians are contented, well affected to the white man, and amenable to the laws and Government. At this very moment the Lieutenant-Governor of Manitoba has gone on a distant expedition in order to make a treaty with the tribes to the northward of the Saskatchewan. Last year he made two treaties with the Chippewas and Crees; next year it has been arranged that he should make a treaty with the Blackfeet, and when this has been done the British Crown shall have acquired a title to every acre that lies between Lake Superior and the top of the Rocky Mountains. But in British Columbia, except in a few acres where under the jurisdiction of the Hudson's Bay Company or under the auspices of Sir James Douglas, a similar practice has been adopted, the British Columbian Government has always assumed that the fee simple in, as well as the sovereignty over, land resided in the Queen. Acting upon this principle they have granted extensive grazing leases, and otherwise so dealt with various sections of the country as greatly to restrict or interfere with the prescriptive rights of the Queen's Indian subjects. As a consequence, there has come to exist a very unsatisfactory feeling amongst the Indian population. Intimation of this reached me at Ottawa two or three years ago, and since I have come into the Province my misgivings on the subject have been confirmed. Now, I confess, I consider that our Indian fellow-subjects are entitled to exactly the same civil rights under the law as are possessed by the white population, and that if an Indian can prove a prescriptive right of way to a fishing station, or a right of way of any other kind, that that right should no more be ignored than if it was the case of a white man. I am well aware that among the coast Indians the land question does not present the same characteristics as in other parts of Canada, or as it does in the grass countries of the interior of the Province, but I also have been able to understand that in these latter districts it may be even more necessary to deal justly and liberally with the Indian in regard to his land rights than on the prairies of the North-west. I am very happy to think that the British Columbian Government should have recognised the necessity of assisting the Dominion Government in ameliorating the present condition of affairs in this respect, and that it has agreed to the creation of a joint Commission for the purpose of putting the interests of the Indian population on a more satisfactory footing. Of course in what I have said I do not mean that, in our desire to be humane and to act justly, we should do anything unreasonable or Quixotic, or that rights already acquired by white men should be inconsiderately invaded or recalled; but I would venture to put the Government of British Columbia on its guard against the fatal eventualities which might rise should a sense of injustice provoke the Indian population to violence or into a collision with our scattered settlers.

Probably there has gone forth amongst them very incorrect and exaggerated information of the warlike achievements of their brethren in Dakotah, and their uneducated minds are incapable of calculating chances. Of course there is no danger of any serious or permanent revolt, but it must be remembered that even an accidental collision in which blood was shed might have a most disastrous effect upon our present satisfactory relations with the warlike tribes in the North-west, whose amity and adhesion to our system of Government is so essential to the progress of the Pacific Railway, and I make this appeal, as I may call it, with all the more earnestness, since I have convinced myself of the degree to which, if properly dealt with, the Indian population might be made to contribute to the development of the wealth and resources of the Province. I have now seen them in all phases of their existence, from the half naked savage, perched like a bird, of prey in a red blanket upon a rock trying to catch his miserable dinner of fish, to the neat Indian maiden in Mr. Duncan's school at Metlakatlah, as modest and as well-dressed as any clergyman's daughter in an English parish, or to the shrewd horse-riding Siwash of the Thompson Valley, with his racers in training for the Ashcroft stakes, and as proud of his stackyard and turnip field as a British squire. In his first condition it is evident he is scarcely a producer or consumer; in his second he is eminently both; and in proportion as he can be raised to the higher level of civilization, will be the degree to which he will contribute to the vital energies of the Province. What you want are not resources, but human beings to develop them and to consume them. Raise your thirty thousand Indians to the level Mr. Duncan has taught us they can be brought, and consider what an enormous amount of vital power you will have added to your present strength. But I must not keep you longer. I thank you most heartily for your patience and attention. Most earnestly do I desire the accomplishment of all your aspirations, and if ever I have the good fortune to come to British Columbia again, I hope it may be by—Rail.

CHAPTER VII.

Remarks on Lord Dufferin's Address—Mr. Mackenzie—Accusations against the Canadian Premier—Unreasoning Partisanship—Menace of the Separation of British Columbia from Canada—Unpleasant Feature of the Position—Treatment of the Indians of British Columbia—Indian Reservations—United States and British Indians.

I DON'T think general readers will as thoroughly appreciate the merits of Lord Dufferin's address as they do who have had an opportunity of estimating the importance of the many conflicting opinions in British Columbia, and of establishing a standard for themselves by which to measure the opinions, sentiments, anger, favour, ultimatums, pronunciamentos of a community in a serious crisis, a community much disturbed, in a measure wronged, distracted by the jealousies and contentions of the men to whom they have been taught to look for guidance and help, and feeling in their hearts that the only true solution to their difficulties must come from the hand which undoubtedly owes them reparation, but against which they have angrily turned. To know what might be well avoided; to perceive that which it was essential should be spoken at all hazards; to distinguish between that which had been urged in temper and that which was the result of conviction and a sense of injury : to show the true complexion and bearing of a matter without assuming to be a judge, and to speak for two hours, trampling out of life long-cherished fallacies and annihilating fondly nourished hopes, without for a moment offendiug the *amour propre* of any of his hearers, but on the contrary addressing them from first to last—whether telling them unpalatable truths or sympathizing with them in their anxieties—in language and with courtesy that would have befitted the House of Lords, was an effort worthy of a statesman, and was what Lord Dufferin accomplished. He did not permit the many allegations against Canada's good faith to go unanswered. He did not even allow the assertion, practically so frequently made, that Canada was all in the wrong to pass unchallenged, and without any espousal of Mr. Mackenzie's political views, he warmly and loyally defended that gentleman from the charge of treachery and deceit which he had heard laid to his door.

There have been some here who have not scrupled to impute to Mr. Mackenzie motives of which no one in Canada has ever accused him, and to speak of him generally in terms very unpleasant to listen to. These persons cannot say of him, as they say of everyone else who disagrees with them, that " he has been bought," but they find no difficulty in imagining a course of policy founded on duplicity and falsehood, and they interpret events at Ottawa in which he is concerned by this light. Anyone thought to be a political friend of Mr. Mackenzie has been regarded as the fittest person to hear abuse of the Premier, and though the number of these gentlemen—who are such adepts in discovering villainy in others—is small, yet they are sometimes found where they would not be looked for. I am almost tempted to mention the names of those to whom I allude, in order that they may not be confounded with others who have honestly differed from Mr. Mackenzie, or anxiously watched the results of his policy, but perhaps it is unnecessary. Lord Dufferin, however, had been made the recipient of the opinions of some of these gentlemen on the subject of the Premier's treachery in obtaining the defeat of the Esquimalt and Nanaimo Railway in the Senate, and when he came to this point in the course of his speech, he took up the question of Mr. Mackenzie's personal honour in such a way that I very much doubt whether that gentleman's traducers—if any of them were present—will care to repeat their slander.

Lord Dufferin's speech has been a sore disappointment to some who, in spite of their own common sense, if they had chosen to exercise it, persisted in believing that he would make such a guaranteed promise as would meet their views; and nothing would meet their views but the integrity of the Carnarvon Terms. But it has satisfied a great many, and has set others thinking who before had been carried away by the clamour raised by those whom I have once before called the extreme men. For the sake of the Province, which no one can visit without becoming its partisan, one hopes that the question between Canada and British Columbia may shortly find a satisfactory solution, and I still adhere to the opinion I expressed at first, when the hysterical articles in the "Standard" appeared, that the quiet attitude of the moderate men would in the end prevail, and that some reasonable proposition on Canada's part will receive all due consideration.

I was accused, at a Public Meeting held at the time of these events, by a gentleman whom to know is to wonder at, of having misrepresented the Province by saying that the people were divided on the subject of the Carnarvon Terms. I said it with becoming diffidence, as one who speaks of that which yet he has to prove, but I now take the opportunity, as a point of duty to my readers, of reiterating my statement with the certainty that is begotten of absolute knowledge of a fact, and with a certain degree of wonder and amusement at the cool audacity of the few who have had the assurance to carp at the frank expression of a truth which not even the most obtuse of them can longer deny. I will go a little further than I did before, and venture upon a personal opinion, viz., that the islanders themselves will not much longer continue their menace of separation. At the Public Meeting of which I spoke, a resolution was unanimously carried, in effect desiring the Legislature to take steps for the separation of British Columbia from Canada in the event of the Carnarvon Terms, in their entirety, not being carried out; but in the face of this fact I believe that the proposal to separate is felt by the thinking portion of the community to be a mistake, and inimical to the best interests of the island.

This feeling is likely to spread when it becomes understood that the mainland would see without any displeasure a severance between the two geographical divisions of the Province. The Legislature might, if the extreme men have their way, vote a Province out of the Dominion, but British Columbia proper would convention itself back into Canada, taking all the advantages of union to itself. I have heard mainland men take this ground, and on the journey through the Yale and Westminster districts made it my business to learn as far as possible the course of public opinion. At the same time the more enlightened portion of the mainland say that separation is folly, and that it is quite possible that even with the present House a resolution on the question would be negatived. The unpleasant feature of the position is that the two portions of the Province are at variance with one another, and one of them almost hostile to the country of which it is a part. But it is always to be remembered that the whole of Vancouver Island is not to be held responsible for a section of the inhabitants of the city, and that while all, with some reason, feel sore with Canada, the majority of the people—if my estimate be correct—are not to be led away to bite their own noses. The gentlemen who once held, but who are now out of, office in the Province ought surely to be able to find some other issue on which to struggle back to bread and butter.

Towards the conclusion of his address Lord Dufferin took occasion to remark on the treatment of the Indians in British Columbia with regard to their land rights, pointing out that the present method of dealing with them really was—though expressed by Lord Dufferin in gentler terms—an act of glaring injustice to the Indians. It seems that the British Columbian Government, or Governments, have from time to time granted lands for ranches, and so forth, to the public, as well as valuable timber and mining limits to their own friends, without first obtaining the cession of those districts from the Indians. Probably the gentlemen who hold certain limits would be outraged were they asked to surrender these undeveloped claims until the Indian title had been cancelled; but were the Indians to take the matter into their own hands, these unfortunate recipients of favours would be the first to call out for Canadian paid troops and British gunboats. Doubtless the subject will come up for discussion when the Report of the Commission now at work in British Columbia upon the settlement of Indian reservations shall have been received. In the meantime there is the possibility of a little skirmishing amongst the Indians themselves. The United States Indians from Washington Territory have lately angered our people by trespassing on their fishing and berrying grounds, and by burning the bushes after having gathered the berries. The old blood of the " Knife" Indians has been aroused by this, and when we last heard news from the upper country it was to the effect that the British Indians had paraphrased the old saying, and had adopted for their motto, "Forty-ninth parallel or fight."

CHAPTER VIII.

California—San Francisco—Gold and Paper Money—
The Slaves of the South—The Chinese in California—
Immigration of Chinamen—The " Six Companies"—
Coolie Traders—Dread of Assassination—Life in a
China-town—Visit to the Chinese Theatre—A Chinese Restaurant—A Joss-House.

WHEN the differences underlying the apparent concord between the Northern and Southern States of the American Union culminated in that break which is now usually spoken of good-humouredly as "the late onpleasantness," California, separated from her sister States by the Rocky Mountains and the Sierra Nevada, took the matter rather easily than otherwise, and without disturbing herself about the probable result of the quarrel, watched the ebbing and flowing tide of successive battles rather in a spirit of curiosity and speculation than in anxiety for the safety or destruction of any particular institutions about which more Eastern peoples were excited, and continued to devote her serious attention to piling up the wealth that has its centre by the "Golden Gate." Money and money-making were too serious subjects in California's estimation to be lightly set aside on considerations which, however powerful in the East, lost much of their force in traversing the continent of America; and if the East, in its extremity, was compelled to resort, for the time, to paper money, the West too far respected the sanctity of bullion to lend itself to any such desecration of Mammon. The fair round heavy pieces stood piled as plenteously as ever in the temples of San Francisco, and chinked their scorn at the Eastern rag that had presumed to offer itself as their equivalent.

Moreover, the coloured people of the South, though, doubtless, worthy of some passing thought, were, at the moment, the subjects of an interest, and the creators of a sentiment that, in themselves, reflected upon California, and threatened to extend to within her borders. If the slaves of the South were worthy of all this self-sacrifice on the part of the North, who could tell what next might happen? It was within the range of possibility, that some philanthropists might object to California's exclusive enjoyment of the privilege of " larruping her own nigger," as exemplified in her treatment of John Chinaman; and if the sacred right of beating, stoning, and otherwise ill-treating " John" were once interfered with, life to the Californian hoodlum would become a mockery. So California was not much exercised about the early vicissitudes of the " unpleasantness;" but attended strictly to the business of finding, crushing, coining, and piling up gold. And despite the curses and revilings that were poured upon him, in spite of the blows which he received, the law's delays, the proud man's contumely, under which he suffered, John Chinaman continued to sweep up the crumbs that fall from the Californian table, to establish himself in San Francisco, and to permeate through the communities of the Golden State.

The immigration of Chinamen is conducted on a system which, with some exceptions to be mentioned, retains a hold upon the individual Coolie for many years after his arrival in America—a hard and unrelaxing hold. The exceptions are those cases where a Coolie has sufficient means to pay his passage, and dispense with the aid of the " Six Companies" of San Francisco. The rule is—the assisted emigration of poverty-stricken Coolies. These " Six Companies" are established in San Francisco, and have their agencies in China. Every Chinaman I spoke to, and that was a great number, came from Whampoa, Canton, Hong Kong, or some other place in the vicinity of the Canton River, so I suppose there is one agency or more, in that locality. A Coolie presents himself at one of these offices, and signs a contract by which he promises to pay a certain percentage of his earnings to the Company in whose books he is entered, for a definite number of years. He is obliged to find security for the fulfilment of this contract, which is generally done by pledging the liberty of his father, mother, brother, or sister, or all, as the case may be. The Company then gives him a passage across, and is bound to sustain him for twelve months if he do not find employment. As a matter of economy, they take very good care that almost immediately after arrival, he does find work.

But there is another way in which the supply of emigrants from China is kept up. A Coolie trader finds a family sunk in poverty, having sons and daughters, but destitute of food. A son, or daughter, or both, is easily persuaded to emigrate to the country of the Far Kee Qui (Flowery Flag Devil), where money is as plentiful, and so easily acquired, and in return for a present payment to the starving household, the emigrating children sign a contract for ten or twelve years' service, the rest of the family becoming security, under fearful penalties, for the due observance, in America, of the contract signed by the departing members. Then they are shipped across, the Coolie trader making his account in the transaction, and on their arrival in America, the man enters upon the business of earning money, under the direction and supervision of the Company to which he belongs, while the woman is virtually sold as a slave, and enters upon a life of degradation. There are about one hundred and fifty thousand Chinamen in America, of which number about one hundred thousand to one hundred and ten thousand are in the State of California. In San Francisco, there are about forty thousand Chinese, of whom four thousand are women, and of these four thousand, three-fourths are in the condition which I have mentioned. But whether in San Francisco or in the Mountains of Nevada, whether in British Columbia or Boston, each Chinaman is carefully recorded in the books of his Company, and held tightly to his contract. And it is a profitable business for the Companies. Take the " Sam Yap" Company as an example. It numbers, say, in round numbers, thirty thousand Chinamen on its books, who pay on an average fifteen dollars each per annum; a gross amount of four hundred and fifty thousand dollars. The working expenses of this Company are under fifteen thousand dollars per annum, leaving a balance of four hundred and thirty-five thousand dollars profit. Each Company is managed by a President and other officers, two of whom are called respectively, " Bone Shipper," and " Assistant Bone Shipper."

When a Chinaman leaves China, the Coolie trader, or Company, who catches him, contracts to return him dead or alive to his relatives. When he dies in America, if rich, he is embalmed—and known as a " green body"—and so shipped across; if poor, he is buried for a time, and then exhumed; his bones are scraped clean by the assistant bone-shipper, then done up in a small parcel, and perhaps with the bones of a number of others, each in his own little parcel, invoiced to the agent in China, who receives and distributes them. These Companies sometimes exercise despotic authority over John, in regulating his commercial life. They have their own rules, and their own methods of enforcing them. To them John yields implicit obedience, as well as to the laws of the country, when these do not interfere with his Mongolian obligations.

At first sight it appears difficult to understand how such control can be exercised over such numbers of men scattered over the face of the country; over men lost in the mountains, far off beneath the shelter of the English flag, amongst the philanthropists of Boston, or the revolutionary communities of South America. The mass of them speak English; what is there to prevent them defying the " Six Companies," and appealing to the laws of the land? In numbers of cases their surety in China—oftentimes only a single person—must have died, and even where the safety of another person might prompt adhesion to the bargain, it is impossible to suppose that with a race of people proverbially callous to suffering in others, the weight of their obligation would prevent the undivided enjoyment of hard earned money, or the exercise of that independence and protection which are offered to them by the law of the land. The one restraining influence is the fear, amounting to a certain knowledge, of assassination. Each John knows that just as he himself would have no hesitation in murdering one of his countrymen at the bidding of the " Six Companies," for a certain reward, so no one of his fellows will be found with any scruples about making away with him—for a consideration. They are all there to make money, and they will make it in any way they can. A peccant John is invited into an opium den, or a tea-house, or a friend's shop, and once in, the deed is silently and effectually performed. There is no firing of pistols, no disturbance. The victim's head is chopped open with a sharp cleaver, or a butcher's knife, sharpened like a razor, is plunged into his heart, and there is an end of him. No tales are told. John is by nature as silent as the tomb on all such subjects, and the course of Chinese law, trial, and execution runs on day by day, and side by side, with the law of the United States, and no one is ever one whit the wiser.

In Sacramento recently, a Chinese factory endeavoured to continue work, contrary to the rules laid down by their Company, and a notification was publicly made, offering three hundred dollars for the murder of the first Chinaman found working in that factory, and five hundred dollars for the life of the proprietor. A large band of Chinamen mustered, and came down upon the offending store in order to earn this reward, and a desperate fight took place, in which several were killed and wounded before the police could interfere.

Chinese cheap labour is becoming day by day a more serious question in San Francisco. It is conclusively shown that the white race cannot compete with John in the fields of labour. A family of

Chinamen can live on less than that requisite to sustain one white man, and gradually the almond-eyed son of Confucius is elbowing others out of the fields which they had occupied until his coming. He has displaced the French laundress, the Italian fisherman, and he is, inch by inch, spreading over the commercial field just as imperceptibly.

His quarter in San Francisco is becoming larger and larger. There are now about four thousand bootmakers, two thousand washermen, over two thousand woolworkers, between three and four thousand cigar-makers, and fourteen thousand domestic servants in the State of California. Besides these workmen, there are thousands employed in various occupations too numerous to mention. There are now in the city of San Francisco about five hundred Chinese children, and these are the prettiest and pleasantest features of the Chinese community. Everything else about the Chinese quarter of the city is more or less repellent.

An individual Chinaman is frequently almost attractive from his neatness and cleanliness, but as they herd together in Chinatown their mode of life is horrible. They literally swarm in dens underground, as well as in attics. They divide a room into two by putting a false ceiling to it half way up the wall, and in each of these compartments they lie bunk over bunk all through the room, almost like sardines in a box, amidst the mixed fumes of tobacco and opium, and the frizzle and steam of whatever they may have to cook. They burrow under the ground which their house occupies, until they make additional sleeping-bunks for themselves under the pavement or under the walls of an adjoining house; and their touch is fatal to all house-property. It must remain a Chinese den or be destroyed. No one else will touch it, nor will anyone, if he can avoid it, occupy the premises next to a Chinese shop or house. So John spreads himself, and people shrink from his vicinity as if he were a loathsome disease. The police of San Francisco know him well, but cannot control him. His silent, reserved, and imperturbable nature bids defiance to their efforts. They may have spotted some infamous den, and have taken the greatest precautions to surprise the evil-doers, but some unseen hand gives the alarm, and fifty impediments are placed in the way while the inmates escape by the roof, or by some passage kept ready for flight. Unfortunately, it has been found that some of the lower classes of whites in San Francisco are regular frequenters of the opium dens and other horrible abodes of vice in China-town; and this discovery has tended greatly to add bitterness to the feelings with which the Chinese are regarded in the city. How deep that feeling must be, may be gathered from the fact of a respectable Californian journal stating that, if some means of dealing with the Chinese question was not discovered by the Government, the people would themselves solve the question, even though in doing so, the sun should rise one morning on the dead bodies of the whole Chinese population. John is, indeed, a question on the Pacific slope. Bret Harte and others have, in their pleasant way, indicated the animosity that is felt towards him, and some day it will practically show itself.

We had heard so much about the Chinese in California, and had found John such an unoffending person in British Columbia, that we determined to see something of him by the portals of the Golden Gate.

We had hardly stepped on shore at San Francisco, on our return from Vancouver Island, ere we realized the estimation in which John was held by United States' Custom House officers. A number of Chinamen, several of whom had with them their wives and children, had come down from British Columbia in the same Pacific mail-steamer with ourselves. When they landed with their luggage, of which each had a great quantity, they were set upon by the Customs officers and subjected to the most rigorous search that can be imagined. Their persons were carefully searched, and then their baggage was opened and examined. Nothing was left to chance; every sealed jar of ginger or other preserves was opened, their pillows were ripped open, their bags of dried fish turned out on the floor, the women's trinket-boxes searched, and every minute corner of their boxes and those things which their boxes contained were investigated as if the Philosopher's stone was known to be hidden in some corner of the varied mass of goods displayed upon the platform. The examination was so close that I was tempted to ask one of the examining officers about it.

"Is John given to smuggling?" I asked.

"Kinder!" was the reply.

"What does he smuggle?"

"Opium."

"And do respectable Chinamen, merchants and people of that sort, smuggle?"

"Can't help themselves, it's in their nature. Smuggle! Darn 'em, they don't do nothing else but smuggle."

I couldn't help thinking that if they succeeded in smuggling in the face of such an examination as we had witnessed, they must be the cleverest smugglers in the world, and would do well to turn their attention exclusively to that business.

Our opportunity of visiting John in his own quarter soon came. We were consulting how we should go to work, when an invitation came from Lord Dufferin asking us to accompany him. We started out after dinner under the guidance of a police-officer, and drove first to the Chinese Theatre. The performance had commenced a few hours before our arrival, but as it would in the ordinary way continue till next morning, we expected to see as much of it as we desired. The theatre was situated in the midst of a Chinese business street, from which it was approached by a long passage filled with the stalls of Chinese vendors of fruit, cigarettes, and other luxuries of the entr'acte commonly indulged in by the habitués of the place. Refreshment of some kind becomes almost a necessity to anyone desiring to see the whole of the play. Occasionally the curtain rises at midday and drops at seven o'clock next morning, and though one can go home to bed and return in time for the dénouement, the thread of the story is apt to be lost by doing so. It is better to have substantial food on sale in the lobby.

The theatre we visited was a nasty,

dirty, dingy, ill-lighted place, redolent of John. The entrance reminded me of one of those dark lanes that used to run out of the Strand down to the penny boats, before we beautified London, except that the smell was different and the *gamins* here wore a tail. The interior of the house was divided into a pit and a circle above it. On the extreme right of the circle were two private boxes, one occupied on this occasion by Lord Dufferin's party, and the other by General Sherman and a party of American ladies. On the extreme left was a division, forming, as it were, a huge private box, in which a number of Chinese women squatted, smoked, and enjoyed the play. The pit and the body of the circle were filled with men, and all sat steadily, solemnly watching everything that passed on the stage, intensely delighted with it all, but without uttering a word of applause, or giving any demonstrative sign of approbation. The stage appointments were of the most primitive order. There was a back to the stage having two curtain doors, one on either side of the centre, and that was all the scenery considered necessary. When a person was killed on the stage he fell down, remained prostrate for a short time, and then got up and walked off. The musicians were stationed on the stage between the two doors, and were in a manner fenced off by a table and two chairs, which constituted the furniture of the stage. As bad as the Adelphi in its worst days. The orchestra was composed of four persons, one of whom made night hideous with a large pair of cymbals, another beat a drum, a third played a kind of banjo, and the fourth a bamboo and catgut instrument that supplies the place of the European fiddle, and is even more squeaky. But this last musician had near him an arrangement like a small clothes-line, on which were hung a number of these fiddles and his pipe. Sometimes he used one fiddle, and sometimes another, and took a spell at his pipe when it was his turn to count the bars. There appeared to be but only one melody in the whole performance, the banjo playing the tune, and the fiddle and cymbals supplying the usual necessary padding and noise. One came to like the individual who played the banjo, not only because his was the only pleasing music, but also on account of the amiable smile which he wore as he nodded his head in time to the air, and jerked his knee about as he played; and because one could not help watching and admiring the dexterity and rapidity with which his long taper fingers dashed about the strings of the instrument. When the orchestra were not playing, they smoked. On the left of the stage, as well as in the place by the footlights, usually occupied by the musicians, were several large trunks, which were not opened while we were there, but which Lady Dufferin said she felt sure were for the "Props," and which served during the evening as convenient seats for the property-men while they smoked and remained in attendance.

The performance itself was thickly interspersed with singing (Heaven forgive me for calling it so, for it was even worse than the Indian vocalism), and the singers, without exception, sang in an assumed falsetto voice, which came through the nose and sounded as if it had been rasped with a file on its way; but they kept marvellously good time. In fact, the precision with which they sang and spoke with the smiling John who played the banjo was quite interesting to watch. They all sang the same melody, though there was a great deal of it of the recitative nature, without any particular tune in it. This is the music they played in China long before David learned the harp, and, from what one hears of the Wagner operas, the music of the past and the music of the future seem to furnish another illustration of the saw about the meeting of extremes. When they spoke, it was in an exaggerated stilted falsetto voice, their movements and "business" combining those common to the most rampant melodrama and the most ridiculous burlesque. Those representing personages of importance were elaborately dressed, and those who were not, took particular care that their single upper garment should be well open in front to the lowest point that could possibly by any stretch of imagination be called their waist. Obesity is, in China, a thing to be proud of, and it is in the nature of frail man to display that which is a source of pride. Their movements on the stage were stilted and absurd, in proper harmony with the assumed voice in which they spoke, and the hand-to-hand conflicts of opposing generals, of which there were many, were fought with the most extraordinary turns and gyrations that one ever saw. When a general was successful in a fight, it was shown by his tapping on the head each private in the opposing army that passed by him; but inasmuch as a defeated foe made his exit with a caper and a shout, passing through one door to enter immediately afterwards at the other, the victory could never have been decisive. There were several ladies in the piece, all represented by men, and these actors were certainly the best in the cast. They imitated the "get up," manner, walk, finicking speech, and general appearance of Chinese women very successfully, and by their acting assisted us, at least, very materially in understanding the plot.

The story of the play was of a lady, the wife of one of the generals, who implored her husband not to go to the wars. She objected both on the ground that he might be killed, and also because he was about to leave her without any means of keeping house. He insisted upon going, however, and went. During his absence another officer—a friend of the husband's—called to see the lady, and to him she explained the hard case in which she had been left. Thus his pity was excited, and pity, we know, is akin to love. So it proved in this case, for listening to the seductive conversation of her husband's friend, at first with great reluctance, and afterwards with evident satisfaction, the recollection of her absent lord faded from her memory, and at length, like Donna Julia, swearing she would ne'er consent, consented. At this point one of the stage-carpenters, who was sitting on a "property" box smoking, came forward and placed a curtained screen before a rustic bench on one side of the stage, and here the couple retired to whisper soft nothings to one another. The lady's mother, however, being upon the stage and hearing a conversation going on behind the screen, pulled aside the curtain, and dragging her daughter forth, commenced to upbraid the gallant disturber of the domestic peace. He bore it meekly for a time, during which the daughter endeavoured to pacify her mother, but, all other arts failing, he took the old lady by the throat and silenced her remonstrances by choking her to death. The husband shortly afterwards returned, and ascertaining that the death of his mother-in-law was not wholly a matter of self-congratulation, gave way to an outburst of passion, and launched such very acrimonious invectives at his friend that another acrobatic combat took place, and the gallant but guilty soldier was killed. The deceased mother-in-law and her slayer then rose and hurried off the stage, and another phase of the drama commenced.*

---

* Shortly after Lord and Lady Dufferin's visit to this theatre, a disaster occurred which resulted in considerable loss of life. A Chinaman discovered a small piece of matting on fire, and although he was enabled unaided to extinguish it, he foolishly raised the alarm of

As it was nearly eleven o'clock and the end of the piece yet far off, Lady Dufferin rose, and we left the theatre to visit a Chinese restaurant a little farther up the street. Returning the salutations of a smiling Tartar at the door of this brilliantly lighted and very Chinese-looking establishment, we passed through the lower room and ascended a flight of stairs into the rooms above, or rather one room, divided by a centre support and the occupants passed from one to the other according as they felt inclined to sing in one part, or smoke in the other. In one corner of the front room was a party of men and women playing dominoes, a large table of tea and sweetmeats standing close to their side. In another part were two women singing and accompanying themselves by

---

fire. A panic and stampede ensued in which seventeen Chinamen were crushed to death, and others were severely wounded.

beating with sticks on a small drum, while two younger girls and several men sat by listening to and enjoying the music. Round about the room were other men and women drinking tea, or smoking those curious water-pipes which require to be filled after each whiff. Our entrance in no wise disturbed either the domino-players or the singers; the host alone coming forward to press upon the party the hospitality of his house. When this affable gentleman had fully explained the beauties of the one room, he led the way into the other. Here Lady Dufferin accepted his invitation to drink a cup of tea, and we all sat down round a table on which small cups full of hot tea and plates of Chinese preserves were immediately placed. We all drank some tea, and several of the party ate little pieces of the preserves, but, with the exception of Lady Dufferin, who boldly tackled a stringy-looking piece of ginger, they did so as if they feared that the morsels before them were explosive material, warranted to go off on being moistened. Seeing the strangers yield to the convivial influences of the hour, several persons, including two of the ladies from the other room, came in and endeavoured to join in the conversation, and generally to make themselves agreeable. The only person who appeared to resent the intrusion was a half-stupefied beauty, who was ensconsed in an alcove immediately behind our table, smoking opium. She was lying at full length, after the manner of opium-smokers, and was probably just beginning to taste the pleasures of opium intoxication when we arrived. The landlord, however, was very genial, and told us amongst other things that he had received a visit yesterday from one of the Secretaries] of State from Washington (Mr. Cameron). He said to the Governor-General, pointing at the same time to Lady Dufferin :

"That all same you missus?"

"Yes!" said Lord Dufferin. "That is my missus."

"Ah! velly well. You English, eh?"

"Yes."

"Ah! supposee you get back you sendee mi photoglaf you missus, all same, I sendee you photoglaf mi."

"Yes, that is very good of you," replied Lord Dufferin.

Then the topic was changed by the effort of a young lady to communicate some ideas which she had formed on the subject of the strange lady, but she failed to accomplish what she desired, and took refuge in a pipe, which she shared with a gentleman with whom she appeared to be on terms of some intimacy.

We eventually left this establishment, almost overpowered by the politeness of the proprietor, who at the last moment again proffered his request for Lady Dufferin's photograph, and were driven through several streets of Chinatown to the entrance of a long, dark, narrow lane at the extremity of which, we were told, was the Joss House, which Lord Dufferin wished to see. The lane was pitch dark, and one could hardly avoid feeling a sense of insecurity on Lady Dufferin's behalf, though one did not know exactly what to be afraid of, except of broken necks. This, however, is always a sufficient reason for anxiety to a properly constituted mind. Whatever Lady Dufferin may have thought, however, she evinced no signs of hesitation, but stepped out into the cavernous-looking passage, and followed fearlessly on into the darkness beyond. For aught we knew to the contrary, or that the surroundings of the place indicated, we might have been in the centre of one of those dens of which we had heard so much evil. We could see no lights about, though we had now turned out of the first passage and had gained the foot of some rickety stairs, and we could hear indistinct sounds of voices, while our olfactory sense told us that we were surrounded by Chinamen. It was necessary to feel our way along, and to look back to see if the others were following. At last we all found ourselves on a shaky wooden platform, which, as far as one could make out in the dark, was affixed to the brick wall of the Joss House. Before us was a large door locked, and beyond us the platform vanished into gloom. The policeman who accompanied us had apparently been joined by another member of the force, and between them they succeeded in digging out of some retreat a priest, or janitor, who unlocked the door and admitted us into the large, cold, dark, strongly smelling temple. By the light of a small lamp which the energetic policeman had, as he said, "scared up out of that old priest's office," Lord and Lady Dufferin, followed by the rest of the party, inspected the several chapels and image-covered altars of the Joss House. There were several chapels in the temple and separate altars sacred to different Josses. There was one Joss who was supposed to be especially careful of the interests of women, another who took some other portion of the community under his care, and so on, reminding one of things we had heard of in earlier days. On each altar were some pieces of burning Joss-stick, which, we were informed, are never allowed to go out before a fresh supply has been provided, though the policeman whom I asked was not sufficiently "posted" to tell me what would happen if the priest mistimed his potations and forgot the Joss-stick.

This temple was very interesting from the carvings in metal (silver I think) which it contained. Episodes in the history of Buddha were told in elaborate carvings, the neatness and finish of which it can hardly be necessary to dwell upon. But what struck one as being a little odd was that in the priest's office one can purchase for a few shillings images and other paraphernalia of the religion, which, to the Chinese, have a sacred character. In the vicissitudes of a Joss' life he may either be worshipped by a religious Tartar or pulled to pieces by an irreverent Californian. One cannot help wondering what percentage of Chinamen believe in the efficacy of "chin-chinning Joss." A number of Americanized Chinamen frankly own their scepticism, and others, who have still some belief, seem to think that it is a matter of taste of no great practical importance.

CHAPTER IX.

Resumé of the Governor-General's Tour—Scenery of British Columbia—Mineral Wealth—The Douglas Pine—Lumbering in the Province—The Cedar—Huge War Canoes of the Northern Indians—Difficulties in the way of Agriculture—Railway Projects—Waddington—Reception at Victoria.

THE Governor-General's tour through British Columbia is over. The Pacific is far behind us, and by Monday His Excellency will be in Ottawa. When Lord and Lady Dufferin reach the capital, they will have journeyed over more than ten thousand miles' distance, and have passed through many varied regions of country and changes of climate. They will have crossed the rich alluvial soil of the Western

States into the great uninhabitable desert of North America; through the Rocky Mountains into the land with the curse of Cain upon it, its parody on patriarchal life flickering to an end, and over the Sierra Nevada, passing from heat to cold and back again to the warm balmy air in the fertile valleys of California. They will have seen the Pacific in a most unpacific mood, and have learnt that the swell of the ocean has no regard for the swells from shore, but rolls on in the uneven tenor of its way, upsetting the digestive organs of king and cobbler alike. They will have journeyed from the southernmost to the northernmost point of Vancouver Island, have left the mild atmosphere of its shores for the fogs and cold of the territory that borders on Alaska, and stretching out across a broad strip of the Pacific, will have seen the islands so famous on the coast for the savage temper of their inhabitants, and so full of promise of future prosperity, and will once more have reached the mild sea breezes of the lower straits, having passed through archipelagos till recently almost unknown, save as a region through which ancient voyagers had passed by miracle through unimagined dangers. They will have held, as it were, Vancouver, Quadra, and all their modern successors in the hollow of their hand, and have seen in a fraction of a year that which a century grew old in discovering.

And, leaving the seaboard, they will have passed rapidly over country that it took others long years of toil to reach; have beheld Indians whose knife, as it seems, but yesterday was fatal to all unprotected strangers, now competing with the white man in his field of enterprise, and worshiping at the altar which he has erected in the land. They will have seen quiet nooks where crowds have come and gone in their hurried search for gold, and by their own rapid travelling will have borne evidence to the enterprise and energy displayed by an infant colony in building an almost Roman road across the face of stupendous heights, and through valleys whose rugged rocks would seem to have been intended by nature as the supreme effort in her final stand against advancing science. They will have found that whether in the cold and murky regions of the north, or amidst the sheltered valleys of the coast and Cascade ranges, those Englishmen who have left their native homes to found a newer Britain in the West have carried with them into this far off land those principles of patriotism and loyalty that seem to combine in every possession of Great Britain the institutions of her people with respect and devotion to her Sovereign and her representatives. It has been a rapid journey, little or no stay having been made in any place except Victoria, and events have so crowded themselves one upon another, that the time even in that city seemed all too short to do that which one desired to accomplish. To speak fully and in detail of all that one has seen would necessitate a work upon British Columbia, which the reader may not have the time or inclination to read.

On first seeing the country, a visitor's attention is absorbed in contemplation of its magnificent scenery. As the eye becomes familiar with that, one's mind turns to the consideration of the mineral wealth that has been already developed, and to a speculation upon the new fields that yet remain to be discovered. On Texada Island alone, to cite one place, is enough iron to use up half the coal in the Nanaimo region opposite, and in Nanaimo is enough coal to smelt the Island of Texada. All that is wanting is a population requiring coal and iron. In the interior, on the mainland, gold and silver are to be seen, but how much is yet unseen is a question beyond human ken.

But the riches of the Province do not consist only of that which is buried in the rock; the country towards the coast is thickly timbered, and amongst its many classes of pines produces one which has no equal if size and quality be together taken into account. The Douglas pine—or fir, as I am told it is—is of immense size, and makes beautiful lumber. There is plenty of it, besides the woods of the resinous tribe. Only the Douglas pine is at present in general use, for people always prefer to use the best while they have it. Lumbering here would strike a Canadian as being a little strange. He is accustomed to the hard-biting winter with its frosty paths of snow, along which the lumber can be hauled without difficulty. Here a road has to be made to each tree as it falls, for there is no snow that can be made available for the purpose of hauling, and an artificial skid-laid road, greased for the tree to pass over, becomes necessary. There are other large species of pines, particularly one red-barked tree that grows thickly upon the mountains, and cedar grows to an enormous size. The huge war-canoes of the Northern Indians, which carry thirty or forty men, and are hewn out of a single cedar, the elevated bow and stern being added, testify to the size attained by this tree. There is a growth of deciduous trees in the neighbourhood of water, but pine is the staple of the British Columbian forset.

Those who have read these pages descriptive of British Columbia will have understood that, while there is yet ample room for agriculturists who may desire to cultivate a ranche in the neighbourhood of the Lower Fraser, or in the bunch-grass hills of the upper country, the Province is not essentially an agricultural one. The nature of the country makes the transport of goods very difficult, and there is no immediate prospect of a convenient market. The island of Vancouver, and even much of the mainland, is fed from abroad. The amount of the produce in the shape of mutton, flour, butter, imported into British Columbia is perfectly astounding. There is a variation in the amounts mentioned by different authorities, but in either case one sees that the great grazing lands on the hills of the interior, together with the pasturage on the Island, have not altogether proved sufficient to feed the small population now in the Province.

The explanation given for this is the difficulty of carriage. The farms on the Fraser and upper country cannot give up their riches, for they have no way of getting them to the sea. Yet this is the fertile line of the Province, and without it one does not clearly see how the Province is ever to sustain itself when population increases. The mainlanders have always believed, and still believe, that the Pacific Railway must—when all the truth is known—come by the valley of the Fraser. If that is out of the question, they will have to devise some other way of getting produce out, or face the fact of endless isolation. When one sees the narrow-guage railways skipping about the hills of the Sierra Nevada, the reflection comes that the Fraser River people might attain all their legitimate ends—supposing the Canada Pacific Railway to go elsewhere—by the construction of a narrow-gauge line from Savona's Ferry to the mouth. Without some means of communication, the development of that portion of the mainland will probably be left to time and Chinamen.

As mentioned, however, the mainlanders are still hopeful that a location survey of the Fraser may be made, when— so they say—the engineers will pronounce that to be the true way. When engineers and professional men differ about the location of a railway, a newspaper correspondent may be excused from offering any opinion of his own. Moreover, during the Governor-General's tour we saw the

Bute Inlet route only from Waddington harbour, at the head of Bute Inlet, and the Fraser route only from Kamloops. We are told that the easy part of the Bute Inlet route and the difficult part of the Fraser route are both to the eastward of the furthest point we reached. But there are some points which are clear to anyone of ordinary experience. If the railway comes down through the cañon of the Homalco River to Bute Inlet it must, sooner or latter, go on.

Waddington harbour is an unpromising idea. It is a small, meagre anchorage at the head of a long strait on which there is no anchorage at all, and which from seaward must be approached through difficult and dangerous navigation. No ships that could avoid it would go near the place. It will be years before the continuation is necessary; but Bute Inlet cannot be the terminus for all time, and during the tour I saw no place between Bute Inlet and Esquimalt that would serve as a terminus. Esquimalt has one advantage over every harbour on that coast. A vessel can sound her way in for a distance of thirty miles to seaward, and there is nothing but the Race Rocks—which are lighted—between her and her anchorage. During the winter months, the fogs and heavy weather are matters of most serious consideration to vessels navigating these waters, and the difference between a harbour that can be reached in a fog or a gale and one which is unapproachable save in clear, fine weather is so great as to assert itself prominently in every discussion relating to an ocean terminus. By some one, and at some time, therefore, the railway on the island must be built if the Columbia Pacific Railway comes by Bute Inlet.

The islanders assert that so much coal lies between Victoria and Nanaimo that it will be cheaper to carry the coal by rail and ship it at Esquimalt than to carry it back to Nanaimo and ship it there.

They also assert that, the line being built, coal can be carried from Nanaimo to Esquimalt as cheaply as by water. I don't believe it myself, because it does not jump with my figures, but the Provincial Finance Minister was good enough to waste some time trying to get it into my understanding. It makes some of the Victoria people angry to ask why they can't take their lands back again, and with their share of the compensation build the road themselves; but if their statements about the country are correct one cannot understand why it should not be done.

The construction of the line to Esquimalt will add some two hundred and fifty miles to the railway, and will—so the mainlanders say—make it longer than the route by the Fraser. If the difficulties of the Fraser are east of Kamloops, we of course saw nothing of them. Below Kamloops the Thompson and Fraser do not present any impossibilities, and there is a moderately good harbour at Burrard's Inlet. Some people declare it to be " a splendid harbour," but we found an eight knot tide running out of it, and a long sand bank washed down by the Fraser River lying a few miles off the entrance to the anchorage. I don't call that a " splendid harbour," although for want of a better it may do fairly well. Men-of-war and other large ships fearlessly navigate this channel, there being a lightship on the sands. And in the event of a railway, whether of one kind or another, coming to Burrard's Inlet, there will be tugs and other conveniences of navigation provided without delay.

Concerning the Governor-General's tour in British Columbia, it only remains for me to say that, on his return to Victoria, his time was fully occupied in giving and accepting entertainments of one kind or another. He visited the Public School, where about six hundred children had gathered together to present him with an address of welcome. Lord Dufferin made a kind and appropriate speech to them, and gave three medals—one of silver and two of bronze—to be competed for during the ensuing year, telling the children that he would keep in a book the names of the successful competitors, who in after-years, would by their success have acquired his personal interest in their career.

Shortly after the return Lady Dufferin gave a grand ball, at which there were about five hundred guests, and the day before the final departure from Victoria a great gathering took place at Beacon Hill, the park of Victoria, where races and other festivities took place. On Wednesday evening, the 20th September, Lord and Lady Dufferin, with their suite, went on board the *Amethyst* at Esquimalt, where the officers gave a theatrical entertainment for their amusement, and the next day the ship sailed for San Francisco. I believe that, notwithstanding the hard work and rapid travelling, both Lord and Lady Dufferin enjoyed their visit extremely. They have succeeded in winning the good-will and respect of the people of that Province, in whose memory their visit, we are constantly assured, will ever remain a green spot. The people themselves showed their sentiments towards Her Majesty, and towards Lord and Lady Dufferin, by the cordiality of the welcome extended to the latter, and this notwithstanding the fact that their hearts were filled well nigh to bursting with anger and disappointment at what they erroneously believed to be the indifference of the Canadian people, whom Lord Dufferin was taken in a measure to represent. They did all to make him welcome that could be done, and did it well. By ourselves—I mean the correspondents who accompanied the Governor-General—the city of Victoria will long be remembered as the far-off home of kindness and hospitality.

THE END.

www.ingramcontent.com/pod-product-compliance
Lightning Source LLC
Chambersburg PA
CBHW032048230426
43672CB00009B/1525